The Min Police Department

Blue Code of Silence

The Minneapolis Police Department

Blue Code of Silence

The True Story of the Murder of Terrance Franklin

Mike Padden

Contents

Introduction

Before George Floyd, Justine Damond, Jamar Clark, and Phil Castile, there was Terrance Franklin. Terrance was killed on May 10, 2013 by Minneapolis Police Department (MPD) officers in the basement of a South Minneapolis home. My legal representation of the Franklin heirs, for a possible civil wrongful death, excessive force claim, began two weeks later.

Terrance was in flight when he was killed, and it appeared from early media reports that he was attempting to evade arrest. It was later learned that an MPD SWAT team had gone into the home where Terrance was hiding. Although the SWAT team was loaded for bear and had a K-9 German shepherd in tow, the official MPD storyline was that this 21-year-old black male had somehow grabbed one of the officer's guns and shot two of the five who were in the basement to apprehend him. He was then killed. I quickly identified the primary issue: Was he killed for good reason or murdered?

Those Minneapolis citizens at the time who applied common sense rejected this story on its face. I did not believe it. Although I knew from the beginning this could be a tough case, I jumped at the chance to represent Terrance's father and other heirs but approached my investigation objectively. I did not know at the time that this case would involve endless hours: over 40 long discovery depositions, substantive motion practice, including an appeal by our opponent to the Eighth Circuit Court of Appeals, and a near miss for review by the United States Supreme Court. It would involve my legal skills for almost seven years.

Once I had completed my investigation, before the lawsuit was commenced, I was confident that Terrance had been murdered. By this I mean he had not shot anyone and was intentionally killed for retaliation as explained herein. Not some, not part, but all of the credible evidence of substance led to this conclusion. It seemed like every day we (my staff, Chicago co-counsel, and lead investigator) would learn more such that puzzle pieces were put together, creating a strong mosaic of guilt. Of course, our concern was civil liability as opposed to guilty or not guilty since this was not a criminal case. I was confident from the beginning that the officers in question would not

i

face criminal charges or even internal discipline, and they did not. My belief in part was due to the fact that MPD decided to investigate the Franklin death on its own rather than submit it to an outside agency. This created significant conflicts of interest and enhanced the prospect of a cover-up as to what really happened. Having said that, not all MPD personnel were dishonest under oath.

I am not trying to convince readers that this was a murder although I believe I meet that burden. Rather, my task is to lay out how I learned of and solved, with the assistance of others and from crucial evidence, the true facts of the case with help from the massive case file and from those directly involved through sworn testimony, depositions, for which I was typically the lead questioner. I want readers to reach their own conclusions but not until after they are informed of all of the relevant facts, which I believe this book provides.

I learned with this case, and those before and after May 10, 2013, that there are a small percentage of officers within MPD who are inherently evil. But what was perhaps more chilling was the existence of a larger group of officers who would deny seeing evil in the field or, in some cases, flat out lie to assist with covering up the evil doings of the bad cops. Most folks know of this concept as The Blue Code of Silence. As such, a primary purpose of this book is to show how The Blue Code came into play in this case, and I believe that is detailed factually.

The Blue Code conduct would additionally be juxtaposed with the later corrupt in-house investigations that would perpetuate the cover-up and would involve agency hierarchy. There are others in the process we allege assisted with the cover-up such as leaders of MPD's union and counsel retained by the union for the field cops in the crosshairs of a civil lawsuit.

This exact type of Blue Code system was in full public view with the 2019 Justine Damond murder trial in Minneapolis. Regarding that 2017 shooting – a case of accidental discharge – the involved MPD officer, Mohamed Noor, with the assistance of others, was talked into calling it something other than what it was I contend. A false narrative evolved right from the scene of Ms. Damond's death. Due to its parallels to the Franklin case, I detail the Damond matter in this book.

This book also touches on other civil cases I handled against MPD including Ira Stafford and Jennifer LeMay (still pending). Nationally, Trayvon Martin, Eric Garner, Walter Scott, Freddie Gray, and Laquan McDonald are also referenced.

Along with the Damond case, other high profile Minnesota cases such as Jamar Clark and Phil Castile are also addressed in light of the unquestionable fact that all of them significantly influenced the final outcome of Franklin. This includes the 2019 excessive force jail case of Terrell Wilson, another Minnesota case I handled, regarding the Ramsey County Sheriff's Office from nearby St. Paul. That case involved young Wilson, a black male, repeatedly saying: "I can't breathe," a concept Minnesotans and the rest of the world would hear about in detail beginning in May of 2020.

The 2016 Castile wrongful killing, at the hands of an officer with another agency, not MPD, involved a livestream of the aftermath by the victim's girlfriend, Diamond Reynolds. Diamond became my client in 2017. Sadly, that event would result in the murders of police officers in Dallas, Texas and Baton Rouge, Louisiana.

It should be noted that on rare occasion, profanity and other offensive words such as the full "N" word appear in this book. The reader will see why – to give the full meaning of various situations that would not be properly conveyed otherwise. These references do not reflect my beliefs.

The alleged official MPD version versus the actual truth shocks the conscience but assists one with understanding other tragedies such as Justine Damond and George Floyd. It should be noted that this book does not cover the Floyd tragedy in any depth, but it became a significant impetus for me to tell the Franklin story. Terrance was killed less than three miles from Cup Foods, the location of the Floyd killing, arguably the highest profile police excessive force case in U.S. history, that has received worldwide exposure. In the span of a few days, I was contacted by Australian television, the BBC, the AP, the *Washington Post*, the *New York Times*, and the *Wall Street Journal*.

The George Floyd lawsuit was commenced in Minneapolis federal court on July 15, 2020. Both my Terrance Franklin and Ira Stafford cases are featured in its contents.

As of 2020, I had tangled with MPD and their counsel, the Minneapolis City Attorney's Office, for 11 years. The Floyd facts and the massive public outrage that followed caused me to reflect on my years of trying to level the playing field with citizens and MPD, an often-difficult struggle. With my personal experiences, I felt this book had to be written.

Included herein is the story about a citizen named Jimmy Gaines who had the intuition to video, an act that not only memorialized important visual images, but also created audio evidence that would be a key factor for determining the truth. Before the lawsuit was commenced, MPD treated this important evidence as if it did not exist. But for Jimmy's split second decision, it is entirely possible that the Franklin heirs would have never obtained justice, and the truth as to what actually happened in the Bickal basement would have never come to fruition.

This book is written first and foremost for the memory of Terrance Franklin, a healthy, vibrant young man who should still be with us. He was a victim of a circumstance where two rogue cops decided on their own to be judge, jury, and executioner. The cover-up that followed was not only perpetuated by the other SWAT basement cops, but by MPD personnel including those who investigated Terrance's death, all the way up to the chief.

Mike Padden
September 2020

Cast of Characters – Page 1 (MPD; City)
Franklin v. City of Minneapolis, et al.

A. Basement MPD SWAT Team

1. Mark Durand (MP5 Handler)
2. Michael Meath (injured; shooter)
3. Ricardo Muro (injured)
4. Lucas Peterson (shooter)
5. Sgt. Andy Stender (K-9 Nash)

B. Other MPD Personnel

1. Medaria Arradondo (Commander, Assistant Chief, Chief)
2. Cyndi Barrington (MPD Media)
3. Tim Dolan (former chief)
4. Timothy Gorman
5. Janeé Harteau (former chief)
6. FS Brenda Hummel
7. FS Kristin Jacobson
8. Mark Kaspszak
9. Jonathon Kingsbury
10. Steven Laux (MPD SWAT)
11. Stephen Sporny
12. John Staufenberg (MPD SWAT)
13. Sgt. Michael Strauss
14. Juan Valencia (MPD SWAT)

C. MPD Homicide Investigators

1. Sgt. Ann Kjos
2. Sgt. Louis Porras

D. Green Bay Incident

1. Shawn Powell (MPD SWAT)
2. Brian Thole (MPD SWAT)

E. Lyndale Apartment Event

1. Sgt. Gerald Moore
2. Sgt. Katherine Smulski

F. Minneapolis Police Federation

1. Bob Kroll (union president)
2. John Delmonico (former president)

G. City of Minneapolis Personnel

1. Betsy Hodges (former mayor)
2. R.T. Rybak (former mayor)

Cast of Characters – Page 2 (Miscellaneous)
Franklin v. City of Minneapolis, et al.

A. MTC Officers/Chief

1. Chad Degree
2. Geoffrey Wyatt
3. John Harrington (Chief)

B. Department of Corrections

1. Dave Schiebel

C. Videographer – May 10, 2013

1. Jimmy Gaines

D. Neighbor/Homeowner

1. Jim Bickal (2717 Bryant)
2. Anthony Oberlander

E. Friends/Family of Terrance

1. Walt Franklin (father)
2. Anquanette Holman
3. Ashley Martin
4. Sheila O'Neal (surrogate mother)
5. Tamika O'Neal (sister)
6. Cala Scott
7. Bamnet Woldegabriel

F. Plaintiff's Experts/Consultant

1. Chuck Drago (Florida)
2. Richard Ernest (Texas)
3. Sean Harrington (Minnesota)
4. Ed Primeau (Michigan)
5. Alan Rogers (Tennessee)

G. Lead Investigator

1. Steve Rogers

H. Civil Rights

1. Ron Edwards (MSR)[1]
2. Michelle Gross (CUAPB)[2]

---

[1] Minnesota Spokesman-Recorder.
[2] Communities United Against Police Brutality.

Cast of Characters – Page 3 (Judge/Attorneys)
Franklin v. City of Minneapolis, et al.

A. Defense Counsel

1. Brian Carter
2. Sara Lathrop
3. Susan Segal (City Attorney)
4. Tim Skarda

B. Hennepin County Attorney's Office

1. Mike Freeman (County Attorney)
2. Chuck Laszewski (Media Relations)

C. Counsel for Plaintiff

1. Jay Deratany
2. Mike Kosner
3. Ashwin Madia
4. Megan O'Connor
5. Mike Padden (Lead)

D. Police Federation Attorney

1. Fred Bruno

E. Judge for Case

1. The Honorable Donovan Frank
2. Magistrate Judge David Schultz

List of Media Referenced

Other Cases Referenced

1. Philando Castile
2. Jamar Clark
3. Justine Damond
4. George Floyd
5. Eric Garner
6. Freddie Gray
7. Jennifer LeMay (K-9s, Ciroc and Rocko)
8. Trayvon Martin
9. Laquan McDonald
10. Walter Scott
11. Ira Stafford
12. Terrell Wilson

Chapter One

"Officer Shot!"

May 10, 2013 was a beautiful day in the Lyn-Lake borough of South Minneapolis. It was sunny, the birds were chirping, and the temperature that day would reach 66 degrees. Although it was chilly in the morning, by 1 p.m., it would reach 60 degrees.

Minnesota winters can be brutal. Outsiders are surprised to hear that the heaviest snow month in the Twin Cities of Minneapolis/St. Paul is March. Folks in the D.C./Maryland area, as an example, hardly ever see snow after January. Measurable snow in April is not uncommon for those in Minneapolis. So called "ice-out" in Minnesota lakes sometimes extends to May 1. A 60-degree Twin-City day in May was like 80 degrees most anywhere else.

As such, a day like May 10 was most welcome to Twin Citians since it would mean biking, jogging, walking, and recreating around wonderful city lakes like Lake Calhoun, Lake Harriet, Cedar Lake, and Lake of the Isles – all not far west of the Lyn-Lake neighborhood. Minnesota is known as the "Land of 10,000 Lakes." It actually has 11,842 with lakes defined as at least a 10-acre body of water.

The name Lyn-Lake evolved from its east border, the north-south street of Lyndale Avenue, a major thoroughfare that extends north up to the edge of downtown Minneapolis. From that point back to the south one mile is the south border, Lake Street, the well-known four-lane, heavily traveled city street that runs east-west. East of Lyndale on Lake is the Third Precinct of the Minneapolis Police Department (MPD), which would become famous for all the wrong reasons in May of 2020. This Lake Street corridor would experience the damage or complete destruction of over 500 buildings as a result of the George Floyd tragedy. In terms of property damage, it was reported to be the second worst from rioting, looting, and arson in United States history – second only to Los Angeles after LAPD officers were found not guilty for the beating of Rodney King. What set off the Floyd chaos was the conduct of MPD personnel.

1

Folks in Minneapolis are proud of their neighborhoods, but Lyn-Lake is an informal neighborhood, not formal like Lowry Hill East and Whittier, both part of Lyn-Lake. As noted in the excellent book, Lyn-Lake, by authors Thatcher Imboden and Cedar Imboden Phillips, Lyn-Lake was one of the oldest commercial districts in the Twin Cities' area due in part to its connection of streetcar lines between Minneapolis and St. Paul back in the old days.

In the 1960's, artistic flavor came to Lyn-Lake with artists and businesses such as record shops. The borough evolved into a combination of old and new with residents of all ages and backgrounds. In 1996, the Olympic torch passed through en route to Atlanta.

In the 1990's, crime increased, and the Lyndale Neighborhood Association received national recognition for addressing it after achieving positive results.

Music star Prince broke onto the scene in the late 70's, but Lyn-Lake did not have bragging rights for him. His high school was Minneapolis Central, outside of the Lyn-Lake neighborhood. But the band The Replacements, considered one of the pioneers of alternative rock, had two members from Lyn-Lake. The Imboden-Phillips book has a 1983 picture of an MPD officer talking to a band member after responding to a noise complaint.

When Jim Bickal left his job at Minnesota Public Radio (MPR) from downtown St. Paul on that May day, he had no clue his home would become the center of attention in Minnesota media for months. Jim assisted with reporting the news, not making it. A significant media entity, MPR News reaches Minnesotans all over the state.

Jim's home was in Lyn-Lake at 2717 Bryant Avenue South, just west of Lyndale and north of Lake where he resided with his wife and cat. As he approached his home around 2 p.m., he saw a strong police presence. He was stopped at an alley, and an MPD officer said: "We are looking for a black guy with dreads." After about 20 minutes, Jim was told he could proceed to his house.

When he attempted to enter in the back, he saw broken glass on his back door. He yelled the discovery to a neighbor and then walked over to an MPD officer on Bryant and relayed what he had found. This officer stated cavalierly that Jim's block "had been checked already."

2

Soon after that, however, another officer came up and advised that Jim's house would be searched. When Jim was asked if MPD could bring a K-9 in, he said, "Fine. But don't hurt my cat." At that point, he went to the home of his neighbor just to the north.

Anthony Oberlander, as of May 10, 2013, was a 25-year resident of Lyn-Lake living on Colfax, about a half mile northwest of the Bickal home. Around 2 p.m., he saw police officers walking through yards near his home. At one point, he saw an MPD officer with a rifle, and when Anthony asked what was going on, he was told: "We got a guy running around the neighborhood. Dreadlocks. African American."

Anthony would testify at a later date that he "never saw a police presence like this" in his many years living in South Minneapolis. He saw at least 20 officers – all with their guns drawn. He said to his wife, "Someone is in deep trouble. Someone is going to get killed."

On that same day, 21-year-old Cala Scott was employed at a daycare facility in Robbinsdale, a city near Minneapolis. She had an on-again, off-again relationship with Terrance Franklin. This was mostly due to his wandering eye and the fact that young women easily fell for him. Some folks referred to him as the "Casanova of the Hood." It seemed hard for them to avoid his handsome features.

In the morning, Terrance picked up Cala's car, a blue P.T. Cruiser, at her workplace – with her permission. The plan was to return it to her when she got off of work at 7 p.m.

Later that day, after 2 p.m., Terrance strangely sent her a text noting where her car could be found and that he had left the keys in it. Later he phoned, and she could tell he was running. He said the "police were chasing him." No explanation was given as to why. After this call, she left work 45 minutes later for the purpose of retrieving her car. A co-employee drove her to the Lyn-Lake area.

En route to the scene, Terrance had called her a second time. He said he was in a basement and sounded really scared. She heard dogs barking. She would never hear from him again. Her later attempts to reach him went into voicemail.

When she arrived, she saw the streets were blocked by law enforcement. She also saw "a lot of police and machine guns." An MPD officer asked why she was there, and she advised that she was looking for her car. She was then asked many questions and shown a picture of Terrance.

She recalled speaking initially with an older black male officer, but at some point, an older female officer came up to her and said, "You need to help us find him. He tried to kill me." Cala did not know at that time how significant that statement evidence would be – although hearsay, admissible in a civil case involving MPD.

Bamnet Woldegabriel was a young woman who would be a catch for any man. She was 25 on May 10, 2013 and like Cala, had an on-again, off-again relationship with Terrance. "Bam" - the name her friends called her, was a challenge for Terrance. She was someone he could build his life around, but like many young men, the notion of settling down so early in his life did not appeal to him.

But Bam? She was uniquely beautiful, of Ethiopian descent, reminding one of David Bowie's wife, Iman. Smart, a go-getter, streetwise, she was different in the sense that she really cared about Terrance and tried to get him on the right path. It was her influence that caused Terrance to enter Dunwoody Institute in Minneapolis to develop a trade for which he could support himself. A negative factor it seemed was his love of weed which seemed to promote lethargy to the point where he would not be as motivated as he could be. With Bam, this proved to be a stressor, and when he came over to her home on the morning of May 10 (she was working at home), they got into an argument. She then asked him to leave.

In the early afternoon, Terrance sent Bam a Facebook message: "You need to call me." She promptly called, and he told her he was running from the police. Terrance asked her to come get him. Bam's home was only a five-minute drive from the Lyn-Lake area Terrance said he was at so she drove over there.

When she arrived, she could see a perimeter surrounded with cops. She called Terrance, and he told her he had broken into a house and was in its basement where he was hiding.

At this point, Bam was "freaking out" because she could not understand what was going on. Terrance again persisted with the request that she come get him. Since the area was surrounded, this was not possible, so she decided to head back to her home, and while in her driveway, she had a 10-minute phone conversation with him.

4

They discussed their love for each other and his belief he would have to go to jail, but it was not revealed to Bam for what. He seemed to accept this was inevitable and did not indicate anger at anyone for this reality.

Terrance told her that he heard dogs coming into the house. She does not believe he hung up. Rather, the phone went "blank." She called back five minutes later. There was no answer.

Jim Bickal later recalled that before he went into neighbor Peggy's home, somebody told him the cops were looking for a "black guy with dreads." Peggy's home had a south-facing window so Jim could see the north side of his house. As such, Jim could see the door on that side, and it was clear the police had not entered there.

Jim heard, "Come out. You're not getting out." Very soon thereafter, he saw officers carrying another officer who appeared to be injured outside of the north door for which he had the direct view. That door was now open. It had not been previously.

Jim Bickal had no idea, how could he, of the later significance of that open door. Someone who would be nearby using a video device could potentially pick up sounds or words coming from the basement depending on their position. This would clearly be after the time an officer or officers had been shot, and Jim's recollection in this regard would lay an important evidentiary foundation for this.

Bickal neighbor Anthony Oberlander maintained eye contact with the officer who had the rifle. He then heard, he did not know from what source: "We got him. Go, go, go." He then followed a jogging heavyset female officer over to 2717 Bryant. Her gun was drawn.

Soon after he reached that spot, an ambulance arrived. He would later describe the whole aura as extreme and a "highly charged situation" with a large number of officers around the ambulance. An injured cop was loaded in and taken away from the scene immediately. To Anthony, this was an extreme build up of force that he had never seen before.

Had Anthony arrived a little sooner, he would have seen a Metro Transit police officer run around the north side of the Bickal home to his squad vehicle right in front to grab a first aid kit. Just before this officer arrived at the squad, Anthony would have heard him say, "Officer shot!" Jim Bickal did not hear that either. But a citizen located across the street from 2717 heard it and forever preserved it with a device that could memorialize audio and visual images.

Cala Scott was thoroughly confused. Terrance, who she had always called "Mookie" – which was the name he self-applied – was not the type of person who would try to kill a police officer. He had never expressed anti-cop sentiment, and it was her belief he did not hate the police at all, a sentiment with which most young brothers did not agree. Mookie never even used derogatory terms when referring to the police.

Based on what she observed and experienced after her arrival at the scene, it was clear to her that Mookie was in mortal danger – not from being killed by a citizen, but being killed by the police. The cops just seemed too amped up, and for someone who really never expressed fear, the fear in Mookie's voice is what most alarmed her. What had happened to put him in flight? She had no reason to believe the female officer had lied, but beyond that, the police were not telling her anything.

At around 3:25 p.m., an officer placed Cala and her companion into the back of a squad. She was again asked, "You need to tell us where he is." Cala had no idea where he was. After about five minutes, she heard out of the squad radio, "Shots fired. Suspect down." She assumed the "suspect" was Mookie.

She began to cry, and as the minutes went by, no officer was coming to the squad, and they were locked in. She was also screaming along with her companion, a young Somali woman. It was hot. Her friend had asthma and was having trouble breathing. Only one window was slightly cracked open.

The original female officer finally came to them and told Cala she would "have to go downtown." An interesting reality of MPD when their officers fatally shoot citizens is that the involved officers are not required to give statements for days due to the alleged trauma from the event. Not so for family or friends of the victims, or any non-MPD witness. Their statements are typically secured immediately without option with a mandatory trip to headquarters.

The officer threatened that if Cala attempted to make any calls, her phone would be taken away. No words of sympathy or any humanity at all were conveyed to this young, African American woman that day by MPD personnel, before or after she gave her statement, even though she had done nothing wrong. Once her statement was secured, it was then that she was plaintively told that Mookie was dead.

It was not long before television and print media arrived at the scene. It was learned that not one but two officers had been shot. It was also soon discovered that the suspect did not have a gun. It was clear this would be a public relations nightmare and was the first challenging event for the new chief, the first-ever female MPD chief, Janée Harteau. She was also the first openly gay chief. All eyes were on her.

Chief Harteau was nominated by Mayor R.T. Rybak on April 30, 2012. Her resume was impressive. Twenty-five good years with the agency, and she once had her nose broken by a suspect. She had written books on personal safety for women and seniors.

In late November of 2012, the City Council approved her nomination. The Minneapolis paper, *Star Tribune* (*Strib*), did an expected puff piece for the November 28, 2012 edition, the same day as her nomination, and even the MPD union chief, John Delmonico, sang her praises. Community figures, business owners, council members, and others trumpeted support. The vote was 6-0. For a city committed to diversity, Harteau was a logical choice due to her excellent work history, gender, and sexual preference.

Some viewed the praise as over the top. Regardless, this would put tremendous pressure on the new chief to not make any mistakes, and the police union, the Minneapolis Police Federation, was guaranteed to give her a short honeymoon even if others did not. By the summer of 2017, things would change dramatically for Chief Harteau as a result of one round fired from an MPD officer's gun.

The Franklin matter would be a real challenge, but something else occurred that day that amped things up even higher. Long after Mookie was killed, an MPD officer rushing to the scene in his squad, sped through a red traffic light and struck a motorcycle operator who had his girlfriend as his passenger. They were both Hispanic.

The operator, Ivan Romero, was killed instantly, and the girlfriend, although badly injured, survived. What made matters worse, was that the decision was made to leave the young man's body in place for hours for the completion of scene investigation. Hundreds of citizens saw this and were not happy. It was later learned that Romero was on his way to send money to his mother in Mexico for Mother's Day.

Those who had followed MPD over the years knew MPD was adept at getting their message to the public in the event of strange happenings, and this was particularly true of excessive force or citizen deaths at the hands of their personnel. But how would they handle this one? Two officers were shot, and the dead suspect they were after appeared to be unarmed based on witnesses who saw him in flight. And how and why did innocent citizens get injured and killed 35 minutes after the apprehension of Terrance was long over?

Although television media was important, it seemed MPD's prime source to get their message out was the *Strib*. In a May 12 story, it was noted that Romero and his girlfriend were injured at 4:05 p.m. Mookie was killed at 3:30 p.m. When asked about this problem, MPD spokeswoman Cyndi Barrington said, "We are not able to answer those specific questions at this time as there is an active investigation into the traffic collision."

As early as the next morning, at 10:51 am, ABC affiliate KSTP Channel 5, articulated the MPD story noting that a "source" stated that SWAT members were searching for a burglary suspect who was found at a home. A K-9 and four or five officers went into the basement to "flush out the male suspect." There was a brawl, and the suspect was described as "crazed." At some point, he grabbed an MP5 submachine gun that was in a sling around an officer's neck and pulled the trigger wounding two officers "according to two well-placed sources." It seemed obvious these sources were with MPD.

MPD released a formal statement that evening: "Fifth Precinct officers went to a Lyndale apartment complex looking for a suspect who had possibly burglarized a residence the week before. Officers responded, and the suspect fled by car striking a squad and nearly hitting an officer on foot. The vehicle crashed, and the suspect fled on foot. The suspect broke into a home on Bryant Avenue. When a K-9

8

located the suspect, he attacked the K-9 and its handler. Additional officers entered the residence to help, and during an intense struggle, two assisting officers were shot and wounded. The suspect was shot and killed." It was not specifically alleged that the unarmed suspect somehow was able to shoot the officers.

Reference was made to the collision with Romero, but not the timing of 35 minutes after Mookie had been killed. Chief Harteau extended her condolences to the family of the deceased motorcycle operator, not the family of the dead suspect in the basement. She added: "This has been a very difficult day for the Minneapolis Police Department and the residents of Minneapolis."

The events of May 10 were front page the next day in both the *Star Tribune* and the St. Paul paper, *Pioneer Press*. Both stories were similar alleging that the suspect had "attacked" a police dog. It was clear these stories mirrored MPD's press release. Of note was the fact that Chief Harteau in a Friday evening press conference (presser) refused to say if the suspect was armed.

The *Pioneer Press* story referenced a sister of Mookie who noted he had no gang involvement but also referenced "an extensive criminal record" – according to the police. This would be a common tactic throughout for MPD – dehumanize the suspect to get the public on their side. Mookie had a criminal record, but use of the term "extensive" was strange. The KSTP story was cited noting the "unnamed sources."

Both papers detailed the motorcycle accident including a picture of Romero's dead body although covered with a white cloth. The *Strib* story had a picture of Mookie's father, Walter Franklin. At the scene, Walter was quoted yelling, "I need to know," when he asked to see Mookie's body. This request was denied.

When Terrance was a baby, his biological mother abandoned him and moved to Chicago. He was raised by Walter and Sheila O'Neal, Walter's significant other and a woman he lived with for many years. He raised her children also.

Facebook almost immediately circulated the shooting. Walter and Sheila arrived at the scene within a couple of hours with one of Sheila's daughters, Tamika. The police demanded that they proceed downtown for interviews. From their perspective, this was agreeable since they were hopeful for answers. This would not happen. The information transfer would be a one-way street as it was with Cala Scott.

Since MPD provided no information on the date of the incident, and none at all directly to the family at any time after, their only source of information at this time was the news. As time went on, it appeared the *Strib* would have the most information of substance. It was also clear that MPD personnel were repeatedly leaking information to the *Strib*, a violation of department policy.

As of May 12, there really was no additional information of substance. *Strib* reporter Dave Chanen noted in a story of that date that the two injured officers were shot in the legs. Barrington advised that once the investigation was complete, Chief Harteau would address the matter including "current policies and procedures."

Chanen's story referenced Minneapolis attorneys who ran out of their office after the motorcycle crash. Although it was clear the passenger was alive and screaming at the scene, no officer went to her to calm her or give her first aid. Attorney Bruce Goldstein said, "I did not see any first aid given until the firemen arrived." Attorney Rashmi Seneviratne noted the disturbing fact that a police officer put a white sheet on Romero's body – right in front of the girlfriend, before she left the scene. She noted, "That really added to the emotional trauma of the incident."

A *Pioneer Press* story on the same day confirmed that the MPD squad did enter the intersection with red lights and siren activated. But why? Terrance had been killed 35 minutes before. The *Strib* confirmed this interesting fact in a Joy Powell separate story the same day. KSTP continued to report using the "anonymous source" who alleged that the officers had been shot by the suspect. The Saturday formal MPD statement did confirm that the suspect "tried" to gain control of the MP5. "Exactly who fired and how many times has not been determined," Powell quoted the release. This type of ambiguity further fanned the flames of citizen mistrust as to what actually went down in the basement.

Reporter Brandt Williams of MPR News quoted Ashley Martin, the mother of Mookie's 4-year-old son, in a May 13 story: "He wasn't a bad person. He was just trying to take care of his son. He had so many

10

friends and family." Mookie's body had yet to be released to the family.

Ashley noted what many felt: The police explanation did not seem plausible. "My son doesn't have a dad anymore. I don't really know how to explain it to him. There's a lot of questions. What really happened?"

Chief Harteau appeared at a police award's ceremony that next Monday, May 13. She apparently had accepted the MPD early version of events when she said for public consumption: "Last Friday's traumatic events serve as another reminder of how dangerous it truly is to be a police officer. Never knowing if that so-called routine call turns into something more significant or life-threatening."

As of that date, MPD was still vague about whether Terrance was responsible for firing the shots that injured the two officers as reported by Aaron Rupar with *City Pages*. The story repeated the vague MPD contention that "exactly who fired and how many times has yet to be determined."

The reasonable question that would be asked at a later date was that if Terrance had accessed the MP5 and shot the two officers, why was the agency so ambiguous about what happened three days later? A *City Pages* reader, Jake Foster, commented on what many were thinking: "How would officers allow their weapons to be taken from them? The police story seems to have a lot of holes. There isn't another side of the story because the suspect is dead so how do we know the police version is valid?" Foster concluded with, "Kinda leaves a lot of room for speculation considering all the crap cops have been doing across the country in the name of 'anti-terrorism.'"

Chanen's *Strib* story of May 13 made clear that the MPD hierarchy really had no clue about the specifics either. Finally, on May 15, Chief Harteau conceded that the MPD squad went through a red light before killing Romero. During a tense news conference that day, Chief Harteau admitted that the officer who killed Romero had yet to be interviewed because he was "traumatized" as reported by *Strib* reporter Matt McKinney on May 16. Many citizens understandably were angry about this. Why not secure the statement promptly when the facts are fresh in the officer's mind?

11

Chief Harteau alleged the squad was traveling at a speed of only 16-17 mph. Witnesses had the speed at 40-50 mph. She also provided no detail as to how Terrance ended up dead and who shot whom. The speculation was that there was delay with securing statements from the SWAT basement cops. Local attorney Ryan Pacyga noted the fact that police interview people "immediately after the incident while their memory is fresh, while they don't have time to change their story."

The reasonable thought was this: If officers in a fatal incident are not required to give statements for days, this not only gives them a chance later to concoct a fictitious story, but they can potentially involve the assistance of a lawyer or lawyers and/or others to help shape or create a false narrative. Whether this was happening with the Franklin matter remained to be seen.

As of eight days after the incident, MPD had not officially stated who shot the two officers and how they were shot. Chanen and McKinney on May 18, solved that mystery citing "two sources with knowledge of the investigation." It seemed obvious these sources were MPD personnel again violating department policy. MPD refused officially to comment for the story as confirmed by Chief Harteau noting that "anonymous sources could jeopardize an active investigation."

The essence of the story was that "Franklin had secured the MP5 gun of an Officer Mark Durand and was then able to shoot two officers named Michael Meath and Ricardo Muro." It was then noted that an Officer Luke Peterson "pulled out his side arm and shot Franklin."

The *Star Tribune* Editorial Board voiced their concern with the Chief in a May 22 editorial. The premise was that her agency should have moved quicker to get feedback to the public for the specifics of what happened. They noted, "But because officers are public servants who can use deadly force to enforce the law, they must be held to higher standards when asked to explain their choices." This statement was in the context of why statements had not been secured sooner.

The Board even referred to the Chanen/McKinney story for detail rather than MPD. With citizen deaths, the Board alleged that that information should come directly from police administration –

and this question was asked: "Why did it take five days or longer to take testimony from the officers directly involved?"

Lost in all this media coverage was an interesting side light of a citizen named Jimmy Gaines who recorded the incident on an iPod Touch device as he was located across the street from the Bickal house. He posted his video clips on Facebook on the date of the incident so everybody knew about them. What could be seen mostly was officers running in the street and around the Bickal house.

But what the media seemed to ignore, including the involved agency, was that the Gaines' device had picked up sounds, voices, and words that would call into serious question the eventual, official MPD version.

Chapter Two

Jimmy Gaines and

The Audio Revelations

I do not recall specifically the background for how I became Walter Franklin's attorney, but like most cases, the first contact involved a phone call about two weeks after May 13, 2013. We soon met. We were on the same page and both believed that the unofficial version that had leaked out from MPD was nonsense. I was now officially Walt's attorney. It was the beginning of a long-term relationship, one that became closer as time went on.

Walt was 40 years old when I met him. It was easy to see where Terrance obtained his handsome features. Like Terrance, Walt was not anti-cop at all. Some people have the belief that all black people hate cops. In my experience, I have found that not to be true at all. However, Walt absolutely did not believe the alleged MPD version of what happened in that basement. At the time of my retention, the official MPD version still was not known, but we assumed it would be similar to the leaks.

Walt was no longer with Sheila, but they were a strong team when it came to Mookie. Sheila was really taking his death hard and had pretty much gone into a deep depression. She raised Terrance from age two. Terrance had the name "Sheila" as a tattoo, something dutifully documented in the autopsy report. Walt had been a hard worker his whole adult life, a blue-collar guy, and he was working for a moving company when I met him.

Early on, our activities centered on interviewing family members to learn as much as we could about Terrance. Tamika O'Neal, Sheila's daughter, who was like an older sister to Terrance, was tremendously helpful. Until we had the official report from MPD, it was not possible to move substantively on the wrongful death case. However, we decided that we had to take the leaks head on and

14

aggressively get our message out in an attempt to try to prevent MPD from controlling the entire public dialogue.

After I was retained, I was bombarded with texts, calls, and emails from friends and relatives of Terrance who had one clear message: "Mr. Padden, you have to see and listen to those video clips on Facebook." Tamika also hounded me about them. I soon learned of the name of the videographer. My lead investigator, Steve Rogers, easily located him.

Steve and I dug deeply into the video. The visual images were interesting, but what intrigued us the most were the sounds and words that could be heard. There were four video clips posted, but one was by far the most relevant and interesting. Thus, began what would be an evolving key piece of evidence for which we would retain a top national audio specialist as we progressed forward with the case. This was all because of a split-second decision by a citizen named Jimmy Gaines. Within 24 hours of my retention, I was on the phone with Jimmy. He was 42 years old, Caucasian, and had been born and raised in International Falls, Minnesota. Jimmy had lived in Minneapolis for years and was currently working at a comedy club and also at a local restaurant, Kieran's.

On May 10, 2013, Jimmy was at 2720 Bryant, just across from the Bickal home at 2717, visiting a friend. He had in his possession an iPod Touch device with video capability. It did not operate as a phone but was the size of and looked like a typical cell phone. Jimmy arrived at 2720 by bike. He observed there were officers all over the neighborhood, many with their guns drawn. He saw officers "zone in" on the house across from where he was. He also saw a police dog.

Jimmy asked an officer what was going on. He was told, "We are looking for a bad guy." He decided to film because he wanted to see how the situation "would play out." He aimed his device right from his friend's front porch. He saw officers running who seemed "incredibly psyched." Jimmy would much later, under oath, describe their demeanor as, "The happiest day of their life with all of the holidays rolled into one."

Jimmy eventually heard sounds that he described as a "quieter boom" and then a "louder boom." He later assumed these were gun shots. He described the scene as chaotic with energy in the air. Jimmy then recalled seeing an officer run around the house and say, "Officer shot!" He eventually saw others carrying what appeared to be an injured officer to an ambulance that had arrived. After the injured officer left the scene in the ambulance, Jimmy asked an MPD cop what was going on. He was told, "We got him. We got the bad guy."

As of May 26 when I interviewed him, Jimmy had not been contacted at all by any member of law enforcement or any investigator from MPD. Based on the comments from his video clip posts, and the fact that television and print media had publicized some of his images, he was surprised that he had not been asked by MPD to give a formal statement. He would have cooperated.

Jimmy had worked at the big paper mill in International Falls, and this had affected his hearing. Other than hearing "officer shot," the booms, and yelling, he had not heard anything else of substance. He had not listened to his video clips to see if anything else could be heard due to his hearing limitations.

Steve Rogers and I listened to the main video clip that was about a minute long. The audio quality was impressive. We could actually hear birds chirping. A member of law enforcement could be seen running around the left side of the house. As he runs to the squad, an SUV-type vehicle, he grabs something from the hatch area. But before, as he runs up, at second 11 of the video clip, he can be heard saying: "Officer shot!" Jimmy recalled that correctly.

What perhaps was most shocking to those who knew Mookie was that his voice could for sure be heard on the clip. On second 9, the name "Mookie" could clearly be heard. Multiple friends and relatives confirmed for Steve and me that this was Mookie's voice. The obvious conclusion from this was that he was successfully apprehended, and the cops asked him to say his name to make sure they had the guy they were looking for. It seemed to be an obvious question that would be asked after apprehension. I had contacts in law enforcement whose opinions I would seek out to confirm my assumptions, and this was one of those times.

We also assumed a fair amount of time had gone by from the time an officer was shot up to the time the officer on the video said "officer shot." This was a concept I would fixate on for months and years, sometimes causing sleepless nights. It would be a long time before we figured this out correctly which would involve the assistance of the audio expert we eventually retained. In addition, the officer's sworn testimony would be imperative, but that would not be for two years. It seemed to be a fair contention that the moment Mookie said his name was after at least one of the officers had been shot.

It became even stranger. At seconds 25 and 26, the N-word could be heard twice with these two quotes: "Watch out for the nigger!" And then: "Damn freakin' nigger!" Just after, at second 27, Mookie says: "Man, let me go." Beginning at second 43, one could hear: "Come out little nigger! Don't go putting those hands up now!" So it seemed also that Mookie had clearly capitulated by raising his hands up in the air. None of this corroborated the notion that Mookie had shot two officers. If he had, it seemed to us there would be words to that effect. Although the cops were certainly angry at him, he was angry at them too probably because of their use of the N-word. We could hear other words, but they were not relevant to what happened to Terrance.

Steve was a smart guy on many topics, but his particular expertise was firearms. He actually trained those in Minnesota to become instructors to permit citizens to legally carry firearms permitted by Minnesota law. We had two big questions: Why was it that the gunshots that killed Terrance could not be heard on the main video clip? There presumably had been many shots. And if those sounds/words were mostly coming from the basement, how was Jimmy not able to pick up the gunshots with his device? It would be a long time before these mysteries would be solved, but our initial belief was that an open shoulder mic for one of the basement cops could have picked up the sounds and words.

We chose May 30 for our press conference at the Urban League facility in North Minneapolis. My associate Karlowba Powell would be with me along with Sheila and Walt. All of us heard the words mentioned earlier along with the N-word with no trouble. As of that date, I had played the clip for at least twenty people, many not relatives or friends of Mookie. There was unanimity with what could be heard.

17

Was MPD aware of this? Had they engaged in professional audio enhancement at this point? Experts in this field were prevalent. Although we would eventually retain an audio expert, we did not feel the need at this time since we had no trouble hearing what Jimmy recorded – confirmed by many others.

Twin Cities' media covered the press conference well. I did the majority of the speaking but permitted Walt and Sheila to answer any questions from the media after my presentation. It was decided not to reveal all that we could clearly hear from the Gaines' recording but to note the fact that the N-word could be heard at multiple times during the main video clip. Considering what happened to Terrance, it seemed clear his killing was motivated by intense anger perhaps from the notion the SWAT team probably believed he had attempted to kill an officer by trying to run her over with a car.

During the presser, the Gaines' video with the audio was played. After playing it several times, I said: "I mentioned earlier the video that is on YouTube was taken across the street from where Mookie was killed. At seconds 24 and 26 respectively, these words can be heard we presume from the voice of separate MPD officers: 'Watch out for the nigger!'; and, 'Damn freakin nigger!'"

I went on to say, "Certainly, it is expected that officers will use profanity in the field, but this is the type of thing that supports the belief of some that racism is a problem that is endemic in the MPD."

I also played video of a news story from 2010 with the local Fox affiliate, Channel 9, concerning Ira Stafford who I represented at the time for civil rights violations that involved MPD. On August 14, 2009, Ira, a 52 year-old black male, was pulled over by an MPD officer for an alleged defective brake light. This was before body cams, but the MPD squads had squad cams also known as "dash cams." Matt McKinney covered it also in a *Strib* piece.

Ira was pulled out of his car for no apparent reason, thrown against the side of his car, then to the ground, then repeatedly tased. This was all on video. He was charged with disorderly conduct, a favorite charge when the police engage in excessive force for no good reason. Multiple MPD officers can be seen in the video acting in the form of a Gestapo-like feeding frenzy all over Ira. They were truly bizarre images.

The local CBS affiliate, Channel 4 (reporter Caroline Lowe), also ran a story of the case including video of a tow truck driver operating the Stafford vehicle onto a flatbed tow truck picked up by a dash cam. Both brake lights of the Stafford vehicle can be seen clearly operating with no mechanical problem. In the litigation, MPD never admitted the lie and held onto the belief that there was a mechanical problem. The case settled in March of 2012. This trait of denying the obvious in light of video evidence would be a common one for MPD personnel.

I closed out the Franklin presser by highlighting the facts of the Romero motorcycle accident along with the delay in securing statements from the officers but MPD promptly securing statements of Franklin friends and family.

MPD's reaction to the presser was immediate. Chief Harteau and Metro Transit Police Chief, John Harrington, gave an interview on a local television station and issued a joint press release on May 30, 2013. As of May of 2020, Harrington would be the Commissioner of Public Safety for Minnesota Governor Tim Walz embroiled in the Floyd matter along with the massive public destruction within a few days of Floyd's killing.

Both claimed that they had "amplified the audio," and nothing "inappropriate" could be heard. They alleged there were no "racial epithets whatsoever." Chief Harteau closed with: "This attorney owes the Minneapolis Police Department, Metro Transit Police Department, and the community a public apology." What would not be told was that Gaines had yet to be interviewed (this was almost three weeks post event), and no attempt had been made to obtain the device from Jimmy to directly secure the video clip.

It eventually would be learned that MPD did not have the ability in house to enhance audio from a video. They had not retained an outside expert for this process and would not do this as part of their official investigation before releasing their in-house investigation results to the public. The video would merely be put into evidence, and that would be it. These two chiefs failed to mention these facts. The video to them was like holy water to a vampire. Not until after MPD personnel and the city were sued did MPD's attorneys finally address it.

19

Harteau and Harrington would never receive an apology from us at this or any other time. Our contentions regarding the audio would never deviate throughout the course of the litigation.

Public anger for the circumstance of Mookie's death was significant, and on Friday, May 31, there was a protest and march at the Hennepin County Government Center, the location of the state courts for Hennepin County in downtown Minneapolis. This was not the first. The flyer for the event alleged that Mookie was executed although detail of the autopsy had yet to be revealed publicly.

Reference was made to Officer Luke Peterson who it was believed had killed Mookie. This was not the first time Peterson had been on the public radar for having killed a black male in the line of duty. Reference was also made to Trayvon Martin who was killed by George Zimmerman in Florida on February 26, 2012. Zimmerman's trial was coming up in July.

I had handled thousands of civil cases in my career, which, as of May of 2013, totaled almost 27 years. (I was 52 years old when Walt hired me.) Not all were civil rights cases, but none would ever be like Franklin in the sense that events outside of the case would assist with its eventual outcome, and this was particularly true with help from the media. We did not seek this out. It just seemed to happen, and June 2 was that type of day.

Strib reporters Alejandra Matos and Randy Furst published a story with this front-page headline, "Few Cops Censured over Costly Decisions." The story noted payouts by the City of Minneapolis, due to MPD, of nearly $14 million from 2006-2012.

Of the 95 persons who alleged they were victims of misconduct, only eight involved officers had received discipline. And in the 12 largest settlements, there was no officer discipline at all. Considering the public shots Harteau and Harrington had taken at me just a few days before, this story was most welcome.

Reference was made to a $3 million settlement by the city to the family of David Smith one month before. Two MPD officers restrained Smith at the downtown YMCA. Smith was mentally ill and in a prone position when he was asphyxiated. Included in the list of reasons for payout were officers who had used racial slurs.

Lou Reiter, a retired LAPD deputy chief, was cited by the reporters. Reiter noted: "The failure to discipline leaves officers with the impression they are immune from being sanctioned even when they know they did something wrong."

Reiter went on to note that cities generally do not learn the full extent of officer misconduct in a case until counsel for the victims have spent a year or more in the discovery phase of a lawsuit, long after discipline has been determined. This would indicate poor and not thorough investigators. For reasons like this, Reiter opined that a thorough investigation of the police entity in question would be imperative. Since MPD made the decision to investigate Franklin in house, Reiter's comments would prove prophetic in terms of how the Franklin case would play out.

A Matt McKinney *Strib* story of June 8 noted the Franklin matter would be reviewed by the Hennepin County Attorney's Office (HCAO) before submission to a grand jury for possible charges. MPD revealed on June 7 that they had finished their investigation. County Attorney Mike Freeman noted, "The position of this office is that every officer incident that results in the death of a civilian is taken to the grand jury." The problem for the grand jury process in terms of public transparency was that it was entirely secretive.

An initial determination would be made by HCAO as to whether charges would even potentially be warranted with a grand jury, and Freeman noted the process could take months. The grand jury would have two choices: indict or decide no probable cause for criminal charges. Nobody would ever have any knowledge as to what specific evidence would be presented.

Officer Luke Peterson was portrayed in the story as a hero for allegedly stepping between the officer who had the MP5 and Franklin "who was trying to get another shot off." Peterson fired killing Franklin. Again, the paper identified "sources" who were unnamed. Nothing was official.

Lucas Peterson . . . the hero. The *Strib* would burst that bubble three weeks later with a Matos/McKinney story on June 30, 2013. This again was the type of thing that would normally take months of discovery and many hours of lawyer work to secure. The *Strib* had it signed, sealed, and delivered to the public and therefore to our team in just about seven weeks post event.

The headline, again page 1, was: "One Cop, 13 Cases, $700K in Payouts." The lead had three sentences: "A woman claimed a police officer slammed her head against a wall, punched and kicked her in the torso. A man said he was beaten with a flashlight. A woman blamed an officer for restraining her boyfriend so violently that it killed him." These all concerned Peterson, a "decorated" MPD officer who joined the force in 2000.

Peterson is identified as the officer who killed Terrance although that had yet to be officially revealed. The story noted that since 2006, the city had settled nine claims involving Peterson, the most for any other officer during that time frame. The story documented each payout in a horizontal graph extending from November 1, 2002, to May 19, 2011.

In 2006, McKinney reported that Peterson and an officer named Mark Kaspszak had an altercation with a black male named Derrick Simmons. Peterson alleged in a report that Simmons' significant other, Nancy Johnson, jumped on an officer's back, which resulted in criminal charges for Johnson. The problem for Peterson was that a city surveillance camera revealed video that Johnson had not touched anyone. Both claims were settled by the city separately for $100,000 each. The couple's attorney, Stephen Smith, who would later become a Ramsey County (St. Paul) judge, expressed shock that Peterson was still employed by MPD.

In 2002, the NAACP called for Peterson's firing after he responded to a domestic violence call on November 1 and had put a man named Christopher Burns in a "neck hold" that led to cardiac arrest. The Hennepin County Medical Examiner ruled the death a homicide meaning a death caused by a human being, not necessarily murder. This death was clearly a similar version of what happened to George Floyd in May of 2020. Amazingly, a grand jury let Peterson off the hook criminally, but in 2007, the City paid $300,000 to settle an excessive force lawsuit as a result of this killing. By 2020, the world had drastically changed.

With these revelations, the questions we asked were: Why was a guy like this in a position to kill Terrance in 2013 as part of his official tax-payer paid duties, and why should anyone believe a word this guy said when later describing what happened? The case was looking better week by week. In the category of "one cannot make it up," John Delmonico, the union head for the MPD union, said this gem about Peterson: "He's kind of, in my opinion, what we wish every cop could be."

Chapter Three
Green Bay

Although we were pleased to get our message out there, and the media and public response was mostly positive, ultimately, our main point was that Mookie was wrongfully killed, not just that some racist cops used the N-word while attempting to apprehend him. Clearly, the use of the N-word was strong circumstantial evidence that the MPD cops were very angry with him, which was a key factor for proving the ultimate point, but we did not yet have any information of substance regarding the female cop who told Cala that Mookie tried to kill her. What was that all about?

MPD had become adept at creating false narratives, and this strategy was in full regalia with the Franklin matter. This concept of creating false narratives would later be used in the Justine Damond matter. Our efforts, and perhaps more importantly, *Strib* stories, were allowing us at this point to control the narrative. Another positive was that other media outlets were picking up the *Strib* stories including the facts of the large payouts for misconduct and Luke Peterson's escapades.

We had requested the autopsy report in mid-June and had it by the end of July. The results were chilling. Mookie had been shot 12 times with most of the rounds going into the right side of the head and neck area. It seemed like an execution: entrance into the right parietal scalp (near the right ear); entrance into the right occipital scalp (neck region); penetrating wound of the right post-auricular scalp (also near the right ear); penetrating gunshot wound of the right ear; penetrating gunshot wound of the right temple; perforating gunshot wound of the right neck; and six others. It seemed clear this was a straight up execution as opposed to just wild fire in the middle of a fracas.

This data we shared with Walt and Sheila. It made them angry, but they were not surprised. It would be one piece of the puzzle, certainly a large piece, that would support our ultimate theory of wrongful killing – and even murder. We would eventually retain a firearms' incident reconstruction expert from Texas. Ultimately, the litigation-related expenses would exceed $100,000 by the time the case was over.

Help was coming from all corners. Even a retired MPD officer recognized the absurdity of John Delmonico's comments about Peterson and commented on the subject in the publication, Ethics in Law Enforcement. Michael Quinn had spent over 23 years with MPD, which included 17 years of SWAT, 8 years with FBI SWAT, and 4 years as an instructor at the Minneapolis Police Academy.

On July 17, 2013, he pointed out Peterson's history of excessive force complaints and that Peterson had lied on a police report regarding the 2006 arrest of Nancy Johnson. Commenting on the chief at the time, he said, "Chief Dolan did not hold him accountable. He sent him back to the street. Now he shoots and kills a man, is given an outrageous amount of time to get his story straight, and the Police Federation calls him a hero." He then cited the Delmonico quote.

His venom was particularly directed at the union head. "The fact that Delmonico said that does not make it true. I know that most of the cops working the street in Minneapolis are good cops, and they do not support lying or excessive force. So, does Delmonico think he is speaking for our federation reps or the department as a whole? I can tell you this – John Delmonico does not speak for me as a retired cop or as a Minneapolis resident. The fact that Lucas Peterson can do what some people call heroic does not excuse being brutal or being a liar." Quinn then referenced his father and other family members who had careers in law enforcement.

This was a reminder to our team that not all members of law enforcement were bad. We did not expect all MPD witnesses in the case to be dishonest. I for one did not have a prejudice against cops. In my career, most of my interaction with law enforcement, outside of civil rights cases, like in regular civil cases, had been positive. My parents who raised me (my father was very conservative) had always taught me to be respectful to police officers. This was easy for me in part because the cops always had a gun.

We knew there were five SWAT team members in the basement at or near the time Terrance was killed. We were also confident the current narrative, which would probably be much like the final report, was preposterous. Would the other cops cover for

Peterson or otherwise stick their head in the sand with "I don't know" type answers? We were hopeful for honesty, but we were more than two years away from our chance to question the SWAT basement cops under oath.

The ever-reliable *Strib* would come through again on July 27, 2013, and it was like manna from heaven. MPD had no choice because they knew it would leak so they issued a press release the day before. A member of media emailed the substance to me. It had the caption: "2 officers placed on Administrative Leave." The media release headings always had the language: Minneapolis Police Department, Commitment, Integrity & Transparency, a saying we would often refer to in jest as the years went by. Cyndi Barrington once again had the difficult task of providing the public with more bad news about MPD. It concerned an incident in Green Bay, Wisconsin.

The content was vague. "Recently, two Minneapolis Police Officers were placed on administrative leave. Due to the allegations and after thoroughly reviewing the available information, Chief Janée Harteau immediately requested an internal affairs investigation and placed both on administrative leave. The internal affairs investigation is active."

Chanen and McKinney came through and solved the mystery with their page-one Metro section story the next day. It would rock the state. The title of their story was, "2 Cops Accused of Using Slurs." Even those who were on the fence about my allegations about the use of the N-word at the May 30 presser, who were too busy to bother with carefully listening to the Gaines' clip or just even with turning up the volume, were saying, "Gee, Mike. I guess you were right about what you said."

In June, two MPD officers, who it was learned were full time SWAT, were off duty hanging out in Green Bay, Wisconsin. They rode their motorcycles straight from the Twin Cities to Green Bay. The story was based on "sources" and MPD declined to name the officers or describe the incident, but everybody knew this content was 100% true.

The officers, names that would go down in MPD history, were Brian Thole and Shawn Powell. In a bar party area of Green Bay, they got into an altercation with black men. Powell apparently used to be a police officer in Green Bay.

26

The story revealed that the fracas did not result in any arrests, but Thole and Powell did not stop there because they felt disrespected. So they went to the headquarters of the Green Bay Police Department (GBPD) and used a racial slur when describing the black men as well as a sexual slur about Chief Janée Harteau, the city's first gay chief. Those cynical of MPD wondered what was the greater sin: What appeared to be obvious use of the N-word, or the term they used for Harteau, which would soon come out.

GBPD, understandably angered because the two MPD officers had criticized their cops, sent an incident report to MPD detailing the facts. This ended up with MPD Internal Affairs and to Harteau who promptly placed both on administrative but paid leave. They were removed from SWAT. They were both white.

The head of the investigation was Commander Medaria Arradondo, a name the nation would learn of in May of 2020 since he had evolved to MPD chief, the first African American chief in the agency's history. Embroiled in the Floyd matter in 2020, for obvious reasons, folks began to wonder if he had the hardest job in law enforcement.

The *Strib* story about Green Bay set off a feeding frenzy in Twin Cities' media. It was just a matter of time before video was secured, and it was really bad for Thole and Powell such that the original Chanen/McKinney story almost seemed sanitized. KSTP, the Channel 5 ABC affiliate, secured videotape from GBPD squads and from the lobby of the Green Bay police station. These were soon all over the television news and available online with print media. The official reports blamed the two MPD officers for creating the disturbance as reported by Mark Albert. It began outside of a bar called "The Sardine Can" on June 29, 2013, a little over six weeks after Terrance was killed.

The Green Bay reports made clear Thole and Powell were under the influence. In describing the black men with whom they had the fracas, one of them, Thole or Powell, said the word "nigger" to describe them and strangely said they were "doing their little monkey thing." When Green Bay officers tried to get Thole and Powell to walk away, Thole or Powell criticized them by calling the situation "a clown show" and then said, "Are you kidding me? We have a lesbian fucking chief that's looking to fire people for any reason." The story bleeped out the N-word and the word "fucking," but the context was clear.

One of them actually had the audacity to allege that they could say whatever they wanted under the First Amendment, and as such, they could not be charged for calling someone a "nigger." The story noted both were in active Minnesota lawsuits alleging civil rights violations.

Powell was involved in a videotaped beating of a man named Daryl Jenkins that settled for $235,000 and resulted in use-of-force changes for MPD policy. The story noted Powell never received any discipline for that matter. Thole had been disciplined for a 2010 DWI arrest. He had been chosen as "SWAT Officer of the Month" twice.

Green Bay media, which normally cared less about the Twin Cities unless the Packers were playing the Vikings, was all over the story too. Robert Hornacek for Green Bay Fox affiliate Channel 11 noted in a July 30 story that Thole and Powell had walked by nine black males, and words were exchanged. There was some dispute as to who threw the first punch, but a GBPD report had one of the MPD cops admitting to it.

Another report noted that Thole and Powell "expected preferential treatment because they are police officers" and that they were "adamant about not having their name placed in any police report" and at one point exclaimed, "You know who we are, right?" Although the Green Bay cops were to be credited for not following The Blue Code of Silence, they did not present the behavior to their local county attorney for charges. At a minimum, disorderly conduct seemed to apply.

McKinney did not miss a beat, and his front-page story of July 30 provided additional detail of the embarrassing, racist conduct of Thole and Powell. One of them said, "We're police officers. I punched him in the face, and I will do it again." After being told by Green Bay officers to go back to their hotel, as they left, they told the GBPD to "fuck off" and gave one of them the finger. The word "fuck" was not used in the story, but the context was obvious.

When they went to the Green Bay police station, the shift commander met them in the lobby. They whined about their treatment, and Green Bay Lieutenant Steve Mahoney told them that if anyone was going to get charged, it would be them for disorderly conduct. One responded that the lieutenant's position was "bullshit" and again cited the First Amendment. The conversation became "animated" and Mahoney was actually concerned that they might get physical with him. McKinney referenced a lawsuit concerning the 2009 shooting death of Ahmed Mohamed Guled whose family alleged excessive deadly force against Thole and other MPD personnel.

A few days later, a member of the media sent me Chief Harteau's media release along with 59 pages of GBPD reports, which were by then public. Although Twin Cities' media had accurately reported the Green Bay conduct of Thole and Powell, there were some interesting facts that were not included. Powell was friendly with current GBPD cops with whom he had previously worked. That evening, Powell sent texts including ones that said, "Hey, Nigs! So I get the cold shoulder, you faggots! OK. It's Powell. You guys working? Hey, you fucking queer bastards. Where are you at?"

Later, Thole and Powell were speaking with two Green Bay cops outside of the Sardine Can. A black male drove by in classic 1980's car with cool rims, and Thole commented, "What is that? Green Bay is too nigger friendly."

After the fracas with the black males, Powell actually said to a Green Bay cop, "Take the nigger's story." After apparently feeling disrespected by the Green Bay cops, Powell said, "This is a fucking joke. They should have run fucking names. You fuckers let the guy go. You guys are all fucking jokes."

When Thole played the First Amendment card, there was a funny exchange with GBPD officers. A Lieutenant Opperman at the scene made clear that Thole and Powell were creating a disturbance by using that word, and therefore, Thole did not have that contention right. Opperman said he could not believe those words would even come out of a police officer's mouth. GBPD Officer Nate Allen assisting heard this and later commented, "I can't believe I'm standing here having this conversation . . . I felt like I needed to break out the giant crayons and start drawing it on the wall for them."

McKinney reported the feedback of Minneapolis city officials in yet another page-one story titled, "Cops' 'Hateful' Slurs Appall City Leaders." Chief Harteau said, "What I saw and heard on the video posted on several news websites involving these two officers is appalling and goes against everything we stand for." She went on to say, "The type of behavior exhibited on the public video significantly damages public trust." The N-word allegations of the Franklin case were not mentioned.

Mayor R.T. Rybak issued a statement noting that he was confident the chief would take appropriate action after completion of the internal affairs' investigation.

Our team knew we would probably never get this Green Bay event into evidence, but we were confident it gave us a glimpse into the soul of MPD SWAT, a group perhaps that did not think too highly of young black males. Would the five SWAT basement cops express surprise when asked about the Green Bay event regarding Thole and Powell when questioned under oath, or would they say something like, "I remember that. That's how we talk"? We were not naïve that we would receive that type of answer, but it would be an interesting area of inquiry designed to take them out of their comfort zone. Any reasonable person at this point would wonder if this was the normal vernacular for MPD SWAT members.

Video. It was hard to get around that. Squad video, a city surveillance cam, a lobby camera, an iPod Touch, a cell phone - it was clear that this technology was changing the public's perception of police officers. It was equally clear that because of the Gaines' video, there was an enhanced prospect that the truth of what actually happened in the Bickal basement would prevail. But we had a tremendous amount of work ahead of us, and an opponent that would do everything to thwart this task. MPD had yet to disclose their official version of the Franklin/Romero incident, but that was coming and soon. And they were especially motivated to shift public perception away from Peterson, Thole, and Powell.

Chapter Four

The "Professional" Investigation

September of 2013 would be an important month with the grand jury result, and MPD finally releasing their investigation report. The autopsy report would also be released publicly. But there were many highlights in August, again, coming from the media. People as a general rule were surprised that MPD did not submit the investigation to an outside agency. It was completely done in house.

The additional favorable publicity began with an August 1, 2013 *Strib* story by Abby Simons. Abby's story, which alleged the Franklin death was similar to Trayvon Martin, had this quote from me: "The notion that he [Terrance] extricated himself from a K-9, somehow was able to access a gun, and somehow was able to shoot two cops before they blew him to smithereens is on its face absurd." I had okayed this quote with Walt before using it.

Since we were confident as a team that the grand jury process would be meaningless, and we knew, for example, that Jimmy Gaines had not been asked to testify, I told Abby, and she reported, that I was "99.9 percent certain that no police officer would be indicted." Even at that late date, MPD had released few details about Terrance's May 10 shooting death other than the initial brief media release.

Simons' story referenced a half-dozen rallies and that Terrance's name had become a rallying cry against social injustice in the Twin Cities. The Green Bay debacle was also mentioned, something that continued to be a huge embarrassment for MPD.

Then on August 2, Matt McKinney came up with another gem. Three white MPD officers, who were with other white men, got into a fracas with black men in a bar parking lot in Apple Valley, a south suburb of St. Paul. Racial slurs were used in the attack, which occurred on November 19, 2012. It was a page-one story. Video, this time from a security camera, picked up the fight. A lawyer for the three officers disputed everything. It did not matter. The damage was done. The

31

officers were convicted of misdemeanors. The Thole, Powell Green Bay matter was again mentioned.

McKinney and another reporter, Randy Furst, then ran a page-one *Strib* story on August 4 supporting the premise that MPD cops had been accused of racial bias for years. The additional contention was that the agency rendered little discipline and oversight. In 2012, the Minneapolis City Council, with the support of the mayor, had disbanded a civilian investigation entity. Ron Edwards, a black man and long-time hero for Minneapolis civil rights, and a writer for the Minnesota Spokesman-Reader, said, "It [MPD] had always had a hostile relationship and history with the African-American community. When I was in high school in the 1950's, we would shake our heads about it."

The story noted the five officers under Internal Affairs' investigations and the fact that both incidents were "alcohol-fueled." Michelle Gross, another civil rights hero and founder of Communities United Against Police Brutality, an organization that spent countless hours for years assisting those wronged by MPD, said, "There's a blue code of silence. There isn't a culture of accountability within the department."

Robert Bennett, a lawyer who had tangled with MPD for years in excessive force cases and would years later represent the heirs of Justine Damond, said, "There's been a lack of discipline for officers who did things wrong." Bennett's firm had just settled the case for $3 million for the mentally disabled black man who had been suffocated by two MPD officers at the downtown YMCA.

The *Strib*'s Editorial Board put pressure on Minneapolis city leaders to take more aggressive action when it came to police discipline. The opinion piece of August 4 was a result of the recent embarrassing and clearly racist events. Chief Harteau stated that there was no place for "racism or discrimination of any kind within MPD." Whether this would come to fruition with change remained to be seen. She issued the clichéd comment on August 5 that "this is not who we are." MPD would issue the same type of comments in May of 2020 when George Floyd died at the hands of an MPD officer.

On August 15, 2013, there would be another police leak, again a violation of department policy, which appeared in a Dave Chanen

32

Strib story. It stated that forensic testing revealed Terrance's DNA was found on the MP5 that discharged resulting in the shooting of the two police officers on May 10. When we saw that, our first question was, "Were there any fingerprints?"

We were not surprised with this at all as a team considering the close nature of the event in the Bickal basement and the fact the blood of Terrance was everywhere. We had already consulted with a DNA expert about this exact topic. It would be a long time before we figured out the perfectly innocent explanation for this DNA, and it would be completely missing from the alleged thorough MPD investigation. It would involve a guy who would become arguably our favorite witness, not an MPD cop, named "DOC Dave." Chanen's story noted that the grand jury would convene that next week. I did point out for Chanen that Terrance's DNA being on the gun was no surprise at all without getting into details. The story repeated the leaked story of how Franklin allegedly ended up dead. There was still nothing official from MPD other than the initial press release.

But the *Strib* was still coming up with positive stories that helped our case. In another page-one story on August 28, Furst pointed out that a new office, which addressed alleged police misconduct cases, handled 439 cases. However, not one cop was disciplined by that entity. But in civil claims, Furst noted, the city had paid out $14 million from 2006-2012. The strange juxtaposition of these facts was obvious: It was only plaintiffs' attorneys in civil lawsuits who were getting justice. Was there any wonder that African Americans in Minneapolis were not happy with their police department?

Before Chief Harteau had her September 19, 2013 big presser revealing her agency's investigative conclusions, I had already received the final report from a person I cannot identify. The written report consisted of 228 pages. The lead investigators were Ann Kjos and Luis Porras. Before the chief ever uttered a word, we had a handle on many of their problem areas and began with our plan of attack in terms of what was done with the investigation, and perhaps more importantly, what was not done.

After receiving the report, the first thing I did was contact Jimmy Gaines. Once again, Jimmy confirmed that nobody for MPD had contacted him at all, and the only people he had spoken with about it, other than friends and family, were media members. He had not been contacted for the grand jury. On television, the image of the officer running around the left side of the Bickal home from Jimmy's video clip became the seminal image for the case.

Nobody from the press, as far as Jimmy could tell, attempted to ascertain what words and significant sounds could be heard, other than "officer shot," which everyone could hear. At least, he was not asked about that, and even if he was, he really could not provide help anyway because of his hearing limitations.

It seemed that the days of investigative journalism such as Watergate were long gone. Certainly, the *Strib* had generated some great stuff that was not just wonderful PR, but information we could use in the case discovery phase and probably get into evidence if the case went to trial. But the rest of the Twin Cities' press corps, although covering the case, seemed to be going through the motions. I had great respect for the Twin Cities' press and had worked with them on high profile cases for many years. I considered the press an important weapon, but one had to be careful with how to work with them. The big problem is that an attorney may have grandiose plans on a message he or she wants to get out, but that does not mean the lawyer can control content. The big seven in the Twin Cities were: CBS-Channel 4; ABC-Channel 5; Fox-Channel 9; NBC-Channel 11; the *Strib* (print media); the *Pioneer Press* (print media); and MPR News – a combination of both online news and radio reports. I had contacts with each of them.

Our efforts to control the message had been fairly successful, but MPD had the evidence, and more importantly, control of the evidence, to create the story they wanted, not how we perceived it. We knew this was a potentially critical time for the case even though we were not yet in litigation with the filing and service of a federal lawsuit. These were excellent media entities, but other than the *Strib*, they were not digging deep. We decided to not go beyond our Gaines' contentions other than use of the N-word by the MPD cops at the time they killed Terrance. We would save that further detail for a later time.

The 228-page report - we called it "The 228," had amazing data for us. It convinced us Terrance was in fact murdered regardless of

34

what Chief Harteau would tell the public in a few days. We now had transcribed statements of all of the basement SWAT cops including a report of the officer who ran around the house, whose name we now knew, and another key witness employed by the Minnesota Department of Corrections (DOC) who would become a key player with what went down. That was "DOC Dave." We also now knew generally what happened at the time of initial attempted apprehension, who the involved cops were, and the fact that there was video, not from an MPD device, but from an apartment building camera. We would not have access to that video until after the lawsuit was commenced. What we did not know at the time was that this video would become a tremendously important piece of the puzzle that would contradict the MPD version of what happened at the initial contact with Terrance.

Almost every involved officer for MPD, and this included many, prepared a report known as a "supplement." Some were as short as a few sentences, and others were multiple pages. Officers from other agencies issued reports in the format of their respective agency. Significant witnesses, like the SWAT basement cops, sat for so called "Q&A's." Each SWAT member had a lawyer present as best we could tell. These were transcribed statements. We would have the right in formal discovery to take depositions of whoever we wanted, which is a questioning procedure under oath and with a court reporter present to memorialize the answers forever. We were hampered at this time in that we only had The 228, essentially the supplements, the Q&A's, and other documents such as long lists of retrieved evidence. All physical evidence, such as the apartment video, we would not see or have access to until we were long into the litigation process.

Bickal, Oberlander, and Cala were right. The police presence was massive as confirmed by The 228 with large numbers of officers involved trying to find Terrance. It was almost as if he was John Dillinger and Charles Manson wrapped into one after robbing a bank or having committed a murder. With Terrance, he was only suspected of having committed a burglary, not an assaultive type crime, at an earlier date over a week before his death on May 10, 2013. Our thought that this was a feeding frenzy was due to our belief that the field cops believed that Terrance had tried to run over a police officer with Cala's car. Perhaps he was perceived as an attempted cop killer. But was that

35

true? MPD personnel would engage in Herculean efforts in litigation to refute the contention that there was a belief before Terrance was killed that he had attempted to kill a cop. The reason for this was obvious – they would be less motivated to kill him.

The events from this report could really be broken down into four categories: 1. The initial attempted apprehension of Terrance; 2. The facts in the basement leading up to when the officers were shot; 3. The facts after the officers were shot up to and including the killing of Terrance; and 4. The goings on after Terrance was killed.

It was clear to us those officers outside of the basement SWAT team issued reports that were completely honest and factually correct to the best of their ability. The most important data was the Q&A's for each of the five SWAT basement cops and DOC Dave. There was also the Metro Transit officer, Geoffrey Wyatt, who ran for the first aid kit and was heard saying, "Officer shot!" But there was also much more.

We certainly felt the basement SWAT cops were not truthful. DOC Dave was a mixed bag who we would re-assess after eventually deposing him. Wyatt was honest and was not aware of his significance until perhaps at the time of his deposition almost two years into the future.

The aftermath of a police killing can be strange, and that was true here. MPD officer Timothy Gorman accessed the scene after the involved cops left the basement and Terrance lay there dead. Gorman was at the perimeter of Bryant and 28th when at 15:30 (the officers always used military time – 3:30 p.m.) when he heard via radio (the officers generally had shoulder radio mics on their person) that an officer was shot inside 2717 Bryant.

Gorman ran to the yard and intended to stay there when he received word that more officers were needed inside. He entered the rear of the home where he assumed the injured officers would be extracted. But when nobody came there, he entered the kitchen and heard yelling and screaming from the basement. He then went to the basement steps and described seeing a "logjam of officers."

He saw a door at the top of the basement steps that he described as "cobwebbed" and "old." He had to figure out locks to get the door open. This was the north door that Jim Bickal could see from his location at the neighbor's south facing window. This innocent act of opening this door would prove tremendously significant after the litigation process began.

After everyone left, Gorman entered the basement alone as he deadpan explained in his supplement. He saw "dark and cluttered areas" and noted "a heavy smell of gunpowder and smoke in the basement." MPD SWAT was also known as "1280." Gorman noted that "after 1280 left" there was only one other person with him. It was Dave Schiebel, DOC Dave, who was facing Terrance's dead body. Gorman checked for signs of life. The black male he saw was clearly deceased. The question for our team was why was DOC Dave down there alone? DOC Dave . . . how important he would become.

Earlier, the day's events began when at around 1 p.m., a maintenance technician for the Green Leaf Apartments on Lyndale saw Terrance at that location and called 911. Terrance resembled a person who had committed a robbery on April 30, according to this man, Shawn Keohen. Terrance was there legally with a resident named Anquanette Holman.

Three squads arrived. In one, was an MPD Sergeant Katherine Smulski, and in a separate one was MPD Sergeant Gerald Moore. DOC Dave, who was a member of the Department of Corrections (DOC) fugitive apprehension unit, a separate agency, arrived in an unmarked SUV type vehicle.

Terrance was with Holman and her two children in Cala's P.T. Cruiser in the parking lot. The entire event was picked up by the apartment complex video, without audio. For the reports provided by these three, it did not appear that they had seen or had access to this video in advance of their report preparation.

Smulski arrived at the Lyndale apartment complex and saw the blue vehicle with its driver and passengers. She got out of her squad and observed the blue car back up slowly. She claimed the driver "headed straight towards me" and struck the driver's door of her squad, which caused the door to close. The vehicle then left the parking lot, and she pursued in her squad. It was soon learned that Terrance drove only a short distance and left his vehicle on foot. He ended up during his flight in a nearby bike store also on Lyndale known as Flanders Bros Cycle.

Regarding Smulski, a significant issue would be raised in the litigation as to what she said about this Terrance encounter over police radio such that other officers in the field would hear it. Her report said nothing about the notion that she alleged over the radio that Terrance had tried to kill her. The apartment video would be tremendously helpful on this issue. We later concluded that Terrance had not tried to kill her, but what did other MPD cops in the field believe that afternoon?

Sergeant Moore's supplements would largely corroborate Sgt. Smulski. The litigation discovery depositions of these two sergeants would not be for another two years. Like with these two witnesses and many others, we would be limited in terms of getting what we felt was the full story from The 228.

Statements were secured from two bike shop employees. Although Terrance acted strangely and said he was looking for a bike for his girlfriend, it was clear he was fixated on what was going on outside of the store. He ended up running out of the store when he saw an MPD squad near the front door. The two employees would confirm at a later date that Terrance did not threaten or assault anyone, and he appeared nervous and scared. The next structure he would be in, as the investigation revealed, was the Bickal home.

We looked in vain for evidence of gunshot residue testing known in legal parlance as "GSR testing." This determines the presence of gunshot matter normally on the hands and arms, but it can also be on clothing. The presence of that material indicates the recent shooting of a gun. The doctor performing the autopsy can assist with this process also, so a deceased body is perfect for this type of testing. The bottom line was this: If Terrance had fired a gun and shot two officers, this would be an excellent way for law enforcement to confirm that fact. But it was clear that this testing had not been done. We would not find out why until we were in the litigation process. We were not satisfied with the eventual explanation.

The Gaines' video clips that were posted on Facebook were in fact put into evidence by an MPD investigator, but other than that, nothing else appeared to have been done with them. The basement SWAT team was unanimous with the notion that Terrance never uttered a word during the time that they were in the basement with him. Then how could the clearly articulated name, "Mookie," at second 9 of the main clip, be explained along with the other statement? It was not addressed in the MPD report.

The report showed no attempt to enhance the Gaines' audio nor was any friend or family member asked about it. There were plenty of opportunities with people who knew Mookie's voice like Cala, Tamika, Walter, and Sheila who all confirmed for us that the spoken name and the other statement was the voice of Terrance. Terrance even had "Mookie" tattooed on his arm.

The other issue from the Gaines' clip was what we perceived as a time gap problem for MPD. In other words, if Terrance had grabbed a cop's gun and shot two cops, it was reasonable to assume that he would have been killed right away, something even Lucas Peterson eventually agreed was true. It seemed clear from our work on the Gaines' clip, that as of second 43, 32 seconds after "officer shot" at second 11, an officer was still giving Terrance voice directives – probably Peterson. And since we knew it was probable that time had gone by after Wyatt knew an officer was shot before he said "officer shot," this gap presumably would be larger. From seconds 43-45, we could clearly hear: "Come out little nigger! Don't go putting those hands up now!"

Then there was also the fact that at second 27, Terrance can be heard saying, "Man, let me go!" As of this date, we had over 20 people who knew Terrance, friends and family, who confirmed that this was his voice. None of our team knew Terrance, but the voice was clearly that of a young black male. No MPD investigator asked any friend or family member about this either. For Cala, Tamika, and Anquanette, MPD had done Q&A's so transcriptions existed which confirmed exactly what was asked. It was almost as if MPD was treating the Gaines' video clips as something that did exist, but they were completely ignoring the contents by failing to even attempt to analyze them. Considering what I said was on the main clip in May about the N-words, this was shocking. They should have been motivated to prove me, and our client wrong, with expert audio analysis.

We believed during this time frame of the litigation that the gap from the time an officer was shot up to the time Terrance was

39

killed was probably at least 60 seconds. Under these facts, that was an eternity. It would be a long time before we would etch this in stone. But MPD should have been aware of the problem based on a report of one of their own officers. Officer Stephen Sporny issued his supplement at 22:56 – about 7.5 hours after Terrance was killed, which was at 15:30, or 3:30 p.m. His report was short – only six paragraphs.

Sporny was located at the rear of the Bickal home where SWAT entered the home. They had deployed there waiting for Sergeant Andy Stender to arrive with his K-9. We would learn that the other SWAT basement cops were: Michael Meath and Ricardo Muro (the two who were injured), Lucas Peterson, and Mark Durand (the team member who possessed the MP5 machine gun).

After they entered, two to three minutes went by, and Sporny heard, "Police K-9. Come out." Then he heard a loud crashing sound, a single pop, and then in "20 to 30 secs., 8-10 more loud pops." The single pop seemed to us would be when an officer or officers was shot. The 8-10 rounds would be when Terrance was killed.

Although this gap was not as long as we believed it to be, this would or should have caused any seasoned investigator to be concerned that perhaps the version he or she was getting from the basement SWAT members might not be truthful. It seemed that two cops had taken the law into their own hands, assumed there were no witnesses, additionally assumed their basement colleagues would not dispute their story, and presumed that there would be no evidence to contradict contentions like the suspect had never said a word. It was now obvious they were wrong.

The Q&As of the SWAT team were also helpful. Each question by the investigator and answer by the officer was recorded verbatim in a transcript typically multiple pages in length that became part of the official investigation. What was interesting, but not surprising, was that multiple days went by before they were ever questioned by one of the two lead investigators, Kjos or Porras. Durand and Stender's were 3 days later, Peterson's was 4, Meath's was 14, and Muro's was 20 days later.

Durand's Q&A revealed that his MP5 was on a harness. Therefore, it did not leave his possession during the entire event. He also had a holstered Sig Sauer handgun. As of May 10, 2013, he was a

13-year veteran. He arrived in a police van with other SWAT officers, some who did not end up in the Bickal basement. He heard from Sergeant Stender of the evidence of entry at 2717 Bryant. Durand was soon at the rear door with other SWAT members. They entered the home in the back into the kitchen area.

Other parts of the home were checked, and the team quickly deduced Terrance was likely in the basement. This was confirmed when Durand heard sounds from the basement which made it seem that the person down there was covering himself with objects for concealment. Stender shouted down: "Police K-9. Show yourself, or you will be bit." They then proceeded down the short row of basement steps. Durand described the laundry room to the left with a door that could be opened and closed. It was dark, and the area was "cluttered."

The K-9 Nash found Terrance, behind a water heater, and bit onto him pulling him out. The autopsy report confirmed dog bites. Terrance allegedly then stood up. Since this black male had long dreads, Durand concluded this was the guy they were searching for. Durand then said this: "The suspect throughout the whole ordeal did not say a word. He did not comply with the loud verbal commands that were being given to him, and he continued to struggle with officers."

We knew right away this was an incredible contradiction from the Gaines' video. Terrance did speak – at least twice. And it seemed clear he had been successfully apprehended since he said his name and later had his hands in the air. As such, we were confident Durand was not telling the truth.

Durand noted that Stender struck Terrance in the face "which seemed to have no effect." Our team would call this the "Automaton Theory," which we felt was a story concocted in a lawyer's office. I came up with this, meaning they were depicting Terrance as a robot or cyborg from the Terminator movies. Although the Q&A did not note this, Durand was present with counsel as another part of the report revealed. This was Fred Bruno who had been the go-to lawyer for the Minneapolis Police Federation for years. We would later learn that the SWAT team had all met with Bruno together before they gave their Q&As. This meeting did not include the injured officers but did include additional SWAT team members who had not even gone into the basement.

41

Durand claimed an officer yelled, "What are you grabbing for? Are you grabbing for my gun?" He then claimed the suspect "exploded out with force" pushing him into the laundry room. Durand said he hit the dryer and that Terrance now had his gun, and Durand screamed, "He's got a gun. He's got a gun." Two shots then went off. As officers entered the room, Durand claimed he struggled with the suspect to maintain control of the MP5.

Officer Peterson then came in and fired his weapon at the suspect "several times." Peterson heroically had put the muzzle of the MP5 in "close proximity to his body armor to prevent anyone else from being shot." Peterson did this at the same time he fired his weapon.

There was one rather large problem with this story: It was a complete contradiction to what could be heard on the Gaines' video clip. And there was also this – noted in a supplement of a Sergeant Strauss after the fracas that Durand said to him, "It was my gun, Sarge." This of course completely supported our theory that the MP5 discharge was one that was accidental, and nobody had caused it to intentionally fire. Durand was not asked about this "Sarge" comment in the Q&A.

We observed that with Durand and the other basement SWAT team members, the questions were open-ended, softball in nature, and never difficult or in a leading form on critical issues. An expected question would be something like, "Did you say anything to anyone after the suspect was killed about your gun?" What Durand did not say in his Q&A was what he said to DOC Dave when he handed him the MP5 after Franklin was killed. That would be learned much later.

Durand was also not asked this question: How much time elapsed from the time your gun went off until when Peterson killed Franklin? It did seem clear that based on Durand's description, the time was very short, again a sharp contradiction from the Gaines' video clip. But the issue of a time gap from "officer shot" to Franklin killed was something completely ignored by the MPD Franklin homicide investigators.

Durand had a horse in the race. If he accidentally fired his gun shooting two of his fellow officers, this could be a career-ending blunder. It would be nice to blame somebody else for that.

42

Andy Stender's Q&A was similar to Durand, and he confirmed his K-9 partner Nash locating and attacking Terrance. He entered the basement with a Smith and Wesson sidearm. He was aware of the specifics of the suspect's flight before Stender ended up with the rest of the team that would enter the basement at the back door of the Bickal home. As a sergeant, he was the leader of the unit for that entry. When he entered the basement with his K-9, he observed overall that the basement area was dark. He used his flashlight for the search. Behind the water heater, Nash "pulled something out." A black male then stood up. He told him, "Show me your fucking hands!" Stender alleged that Terrance just "stared at me." Stender then punched the suspect as hard as he could in the face because he thought "he might have a gun."

He repeated Durand's contention about the reaction of Terrance as a "vacant deep stare." He further alleged Terrance did not respond to his voice directives.

Stender then claimed that with Meath, he pulled Terrance into the laundry room area. Peterson then stepped in and assumed Stender's position. Stender then heard an officer yell, "Don't be grabbing for my gun. Are you grabbing for my gun?" Stender heard two shots and observed that Muro was injured.

Stender then said something interesting: After helping to get Muro out of the laundry room, that room's door ended up closed. This was a bizarre revelation that would prove important to our theory after we began to litigate, but we did not know it at the time. After that, Stender heard no additional shots and only hollering. That was it. He could not say how Muro was shot. He was not aware that Meath had been shot until much later after Franklin had been killed.

Our impression was that Stender was intent on getting Nash out of there because he was aware someone, probably Peterson, was not going to allow Terrance to get out of that basement alive. He did not want his dog to get hit by a stray round.

Muro's statement was not secured until 20 days later, which we really could not criticize since he sustained a serious bullet wound to a hip and was hospitalized for a week. His convalescence was fairly long after that. Like other officers, he entered the basement with a fully capable sidearm, a Sig Sauer 9 mm.

He was aware that the suspect had struck an MPD squad, and then he provided a significant admission: A female officer had stated on police radio that the suspect "almost hit her." It would seem reasonable that this would anger any cop in the field, much less the SWAT team, but the investigators never asked anyone about that topic.

After Muro had entered, and after the initial search above the basement, Durand signaled to Muro non-verbally and pointed toward the basement. It was clear the suspect was down there since the rest of the home had already been searched. Muro stated that the order into the basement was Stender, Durand, and Peterson, and then Muro with Meath behind him. The basement was dark. Since a light switch could not be found, Muro activated his flashlight. He described the basement as "cluttered" with "barely enough room to walk."

Soon thereafter, Muro heard Stender shouting voice commands like, "Let me see your hands." He then described a struggle with the other four officers with a black male in the laundry room. Muro then approached the area, and heard someone say numerous times, "He's got a gun." He did not identify who said this.

At around that same time, he was "hit," meaning shot. He speculated that the suspect was shooting him, but he never saw that. He actually contended that he yelled, "He has a gun," but that was only because another team member said that.

The big question we had was that if he felt the suspect had shot him, why did he not dispatch the suspect right away by shooting him? He claimed that he "did not have a shot." Muro admitted the only thing he really saw of substance was the others fighting with the suspect. In fact, after he was shot, he heard only two or three shots even though there were apparently ten, perhaps more.

And of course, like Durand and Stender, Muro was not asked this question: How much time elapsed between the time you were shot and you heard those later shots? Perhaps he would have said he did not know, but the fact he was not asked the question was strong evidence to support that the homicide investigators did not perceive a time gap problem, or perhaps, they knew and were ignoring the issue.

Our review of the Q&A's of Peterson and Meath remained. We were confident these would be dishonest, but what it came down to

44

was the story of these two officers with Durand. It was clear Stender and Muro really could not fill in the blanks for the key moments before Terrance was killed although Stender supported the absurd Automaton Theory.

Meath entered the basement with a Sig Sauer 45 mm. Like the other SWAT members, he was fully capable of easily killing an unarmed suspect. It would take just a second to secure the gun from its holster, something Meath and the other officers all had – a holstered sidearm.

As Meath came into the basement, he heard Stender giving commands to a person he assumed was the suspect who they had now found. He then said he saw Stender in a "physical altercation" with a black male. K-9 Nash was attempting to bite the man.

Like the others, Meath supported the Automaton Theory when he said the suspect "had a blank stare on his face." He then noted that the suspect made "no noise or any comments." He assisted Stender who had the suspect near the water heater.

Meath grabbed the man's shoulders then the man "exploded forward pushing him back." We felt this was further evidence to support that Meath was going with the Automaton Theory. These descriptions were so strange, and when juxtaposed with the Gaines' clips, which we felt made clear Terrance had been successfully apprehended, and had spoken, alone made Meath's description not credible.

Meath went on: He was applying "knee strikes" when he observed that the suspect was now in an altercation with Peterson and Durand. Meath alleged the suspect lunged at Durand, forcing Durand into the laundry room. Meath made clear he had trouble seeing because the area was "extremely dark."

Meath heard a loud bang, and then someone yelled, he did not identify who, "He's got a gun." He then immediately noticed pain in his right thigh and hip area. He then was in a seated position and heard a struggle to his left. He saw Peterson on top of the suspect. They were struggling over "something" between the two bodies. Meath then deduced it was the gun that somebody said the suspect had control of.

Meath said he was scared and felt he "would die in that basement." He barely recalled shooting his gun but saw the suspect go limp against Peterson's body. After, Peterson and Durand carried Meath up the basement steps and out the "side door located at the top of the steps." This was further important corroboration that the north-side door was open for the purpose of removing the injured officers. And it was clear that the removal of Muro earlier was quick.

Perhaps what was most interesting about Meath's Q&A was that he had no idea how he ended up getting shot. Although he alleged that he heard something that would make one think it was the suspect, he had not seen how he was shot. His contention that he knew right away he had been shot would later be contested.

Lucas Peterson, Badge #5630. His Q&A was left. We knew it would be full of untruths, but would he paint himself out to be a hero? We felt this man was the prime mover with the killing of Terrance. It was assumed his story would mirror that of Durand, and interestingly, his Q&A was one day after Durand's. Did his lawyer have a hard copy of the statement and brief Peterson before his Q&A? It appeared both had the same lawyer so that seemed likely.

Had Peterson's checkered history caused intense anger toward black people? Did he have an issue with black people before he suffocated Chris Burns to death in 2002? Why was he not fired then? Why was he not fired for the Nancy Johnson incident in 2006?

Although Stender, Meath, and Muro had heard the "he's got a gun" statement, or words to that effect, they really could not say at all who was responsible for the MP5 discharging. Maybe this was a way to assuage their guilt for the whole situation, but the Blue Code would not completely abandon them.

Peterson's Q&A was taken by Sergeant Ann Kjos at 4:15 p.m. on May 14, 2013. This was the last one of the three uninjured SWAT members. He had counsel present.

His employment began in June of 1999. He was not asked about the Burns' killing in 2002 nor about the Johnson matter in 2006 when Peterson's report resulted in an innocent black woman being criminally charged.

Peterson's side arm on May 10 was a Sig Sauer. It was loaded with a 20-round magazine, with one more in the chamber. Peterson knew from radio traffic that the suspect had "rammed" a marked squad. He learned of the broken back door at 2717 Bryant, went there, and soon the others were with him.

He described the search of the home, which left lastly the basement. Durand was at the top of the basement steps, and whispered to Peterson, "He's down there." Peterson noted that Stender went into the basement first with K-9 Nash. Nash had the Bickal cat in his mouth. The dog released the cat, and it ran upstairs. Peterson was behind Stender, and then Muro and Meath joined. He noted the laundry room on his left side, and an overall "dark basement." Peterson described himself as the "cover officer" for Stender. The suspect was found behind the water heater by Nash, who was biting him. The suspect "stood then and would not come out." With another version of the Automaton Theory, Peterson said, "I could tell he appeared immune to pain from a dog bite and was not phased by our presence or commands. He appeared almost vacant during this entire confrontation." It was more nonsense.

Durand was to Peterson's right, one step into the laundry room. Stender gave the command to "show hands," and Peterson described the suspect as "non-compliant." He witnessed Stender give a hard punch to the suspect's face. Peterson "watched in amazement as the suspect had no reaction, as if he did not feel it." Stender then struck the suspect with his flashlight, and the suspect began to bleed from his face.

Peterson then heard an officer yell, "What are you grabbing at? Are you grabbing my gun?" He then described the suspect throwing punches wildly. The suspect then charged at Peterson, "like a bull," knocking him into a wall. Peterson described that the black male hit Durand like "a football player tackles someone." Peterson further alleged Franklin drove Durand into the laundry room. He recalled hearing a loud bang by the dryer. He alleged Franklin and Durand were "fighting."

Just then, Muro and Meath both yelled out that they had been shot. Peterson admitted not hearing the shots or seeing muzzle flash. He did, however, hear Durand yell that the suspect had a gun. The flashlight mounted on the MP5 came on when the suspect was on Durand.

Peterson alleged Franklin had control of the pistol grip. The suspect was "scanning the room," and Peterson alleged the flashlight beam was on him. Peterson alleged Franklin was using the flashlight "to find an officer to shoot at." Our team viewed this comment as particularly strange bordering on laughable.

Peterson then claimed that he used his bulletproof vest as a "body bunker" for those behind him. His heroism was now confirmed, we thought. Peterson was able to secure his sidearm and shot the suspect, he recalled, "2 to 4 times." He saw Meath was shooting the suspect also. The shots of both were described by Peterson to be in "close succession."

Interestingly, without specifically being asked, he opined that the time from the two officers being shot to the suspect being shot was "no longer than seconds." From Peterson's description, it was clear the MP5, and therefore Durand, were right in the middle of the fracas. This was an important fact for our eventual theory.

Peterson rendered first aid to the injured officers. He then provided the interesting fact that the door of the laundry room was closed. He claimed Durand opened the door for him. We would eventually conclude that Durand was not in that room when that door was opened.

Peterson later checked the suspect and described "massive head trauma." Peterson noted that he, Peterson, was covered in blood – hands, arms, uniform, face, and hair. This was another huge admission that would tie into the forensic analysis of the MP5, which we would address at a later date.

According to Peterson's story, he was not only a hero, but he was the prime mover in rendering first aid to the injured officers before the EMTs arrived. He said nothing about Terrance speaking. From Peterson's description, there was no indication that Terrance had been taken into custody. There was nothing about Terrance raising his hands in response to any voice directive. Peterson said nothing about: "Come out little nigger! Don't go putting those hands up now!" Who had said that? We thought it was probably Peterson.

Every single basement SWAT member, all five, had a story that could not be successfully juxtaposed with what could be heard on the Gaines' video clip. This was a major problem for the police investigation, and the lead investigators, we believed, had to know that.

Under Minnesota law, grand jury proceedings are secretive. We would never know then, and still do not know as of this date, what evidence was presented to the grand jurors regarding the killing of Terrance Franklin. We were, however, able to figure out some of what we knew they did not see – or hear.

The announcement came on September 19, 2013, published in both the *Pioneer Press* and *Strib* the next day, that a grand jury had cleared Minneapolis police of wrongdoing in the May shooting. County Attorney, Mike Freeman, said, "The criminal process is now complete." Freeman went on to say that the investigation by MPD was "a professional investigation, thorough and complete."

Both stories highlighted The 228. Chief Harteau additionally held a press conference on that same September day. She emphasized what she believed was the important evidence supporting the conclusion that her officers did nothing wrong. She did extend her sympathies to Walter and Sheila, but she made this major point: "Terrance Franklin's actions dictated the outcome on May 10." She was grateful that the two injured officers survived their wounds.

I was quoted throughout the *Pioneer Press* story. David Hanners was a reporter I knew well from the 2009 Fong Lee case, the controversial killing of a young Asian male by an MPD officer. I was lead counsel on that case. I repeated for the record that we never expected an indictment, but the bottom line was that this was one of the times where we just had to take it. This was MPD's show because they had control of the evidence.

However, *Strib* reporter McKinney ran a story one day later that highlighted the autopsy report, which by then had been released publicly, and noted that Terrance had been shot 10 times. The 228 claimed Terrance had been shot eight times. MPD had not immediately responded when McKinney asked them to "explain the discrepancy." I was given several quotes in the story. Normally, a lawyer is fortunate to get even one quote in. Even at this late date, we were still getting our message out. I said, "What's he going to do? Kill 5 guys in the basement and go out and face the army outside?" The *Strib* stories were always objective, but the reporters were almost like they became a member of our team. We often said within our team: "Thank God for freedom of the press."

49

I noted Harteau's presser had Terrance described as a "burglary suspect." That accusation had never been proven, and Terrance would never have his day in court for obvious reasons. I noted to media that Terrance was "very scared." We knew that from Bam and Cala, but not one word was mentioned about that by Chief Harteau. I closed with, "They were saying they were shooting to kill because he had shot a gun. I don't agree that he shot a gun."

MPD was sure everything was copacetic. But was it? It would take the civil litigation discovery process to get the truth out. And it was not just because of the Gaines' video. There was a great deal of other evidence, right in their own investigation, that made clear MPD had major problems with their official story. It was time to litigate, but we had just learned of another interesting fact about the MP5.

Chapter Five

Where's the Blood?

We had good facts. What we had seen was chilling. It seemed obvious to us that Terrance had been murdered, but we had to prove that. Although the world was significantly changing, Minnesotans at least historically tended to be pro cop, and Minnesota juries in state and federal court tended to be all white or mostly white, which alone does not mean they would rule against the family of a black male. However, African Americans as a general rule were more inclined to not believe the police. We did feel that a competent juror, unbiased, with the right facts, would certainly rule against the police regardless of their race, and we felt like we were close if not already there.

After the dust settled from all of the 2013 media reports, the grand jury, and Chief Harteau's September presser – which made it seem that the killing of Terrance was clean, we stumbled across something in The 228 that we perceived as incredibly important. It supported the Gaines' video clip and confirmed our claim that Terrance surrendered and was easily apprehended after K-9 Nash pulled him out from behind the water heater.

The MP5 that Durand possessed on May 10, 2013 was a submachine gun developed in the 1960's by a manufacturer from West Germany known as Heckler & Koch. Viewed as arguably the most popular submachine gun, and used by security and military forces worldwide, it functioned with a semi-automatic feature. Semi-automatic means the ability to fire one shot every time the trigger is pulled. With an automatic weapon, the firearm fires continually until the trigger is released. The origin of the name was "machine pistol," and the manufacturer came up with the nomenclature or model known as "Mazda Protégé 5."

A supplement of an Officer Jonathon Kingsbury revealed some bizarre facts about this interesting firearm. We had yet to learn of the strange history of the MP5 in the minutes after Terrance was killed,

51

but at some point, Stender ended up with it and placed it in the trunk of Kingsbury's squad. Strangely, Durand, who was with Kingsbury, had the handgun Meath used to kill Franklin. No reports at this time indicated that any of these men were wearing gloves.

Kingsbury was in the mix because he was designated as the "escort officer" for Durand, and in this capacity, Kingsbury would basically be the officer's shadow after the critical incident before that officer would be dismissed from his duties for the day.

But then, Kingsbury "drove out of the perimeter" before the crime lab technicians known as "FS," forensic scientists, had arrived. Kingsbury left the scene without permission with two of the three guns involved in this critical incident shooting!

Cooler heads prevailed, and Sgt. Porras told Kingsbury to get back to the scene and have "Car 21" (the crime-lab scene vehicle) recover both firearms. Our team often joked that we would have liked to have been a fly on the wall for that conversation. Had there been a transcription, we were guessing expletives would have been deleted.

For homicides, it is normal for MPD crime lab personnel to arrive at scenes and to "process" the scene. The Franklin case was clearly in the category of homicide meaning that the deceased person was killed at the hands of a human or humans. Murder is a separate assessment. That was of course what we were trying to prove. Was Terrance legitimately killed, or was he murdered?

FS Kristin Jacobson was working the scene that day with a trainee, FS Brenda Hummel. As time went on with our investigation, we felt those trained in science, such as the medical doctor who performed the autopsy, issued honest, objective reports which we felt were 100% legitimate to the best of their ability. This included the MPD crime scene folks. When they saw the MP5 in Kingsbury's trunk, Jacobson took pictures of it. Pictures were also taken later at the crime lab.

Hummel then took the gun out of the trunk, which Jacobson observed. When both had arrived earlier, they actually had entered the basement and saw Terrance's deceased body in place in the basement laundry room along with blood that was everywhere especially under Terrance's head.

When we thought of this case and how Terrance was killed, it seemed to be essentially execution-style. I, and others on our team, had thought of the famous, seminal image from the Vietnam era when a South Vietnamese officer shot a Vietcong soldier at the right temple. The blood came out like a sieve. Terrance had more than one shot to the head, the ear, the temple, etcetera. There had to be blood everywhere, and there was. Even Lucas Peterson would eventually agree with that

Hummel's work at the scene was documented in a four-page report, Supplement #81. Her activities were many including rounding up and locating all shell casings known as "DCCs." She would also dutifully note the location of blood on objects such as areas of blood in the small laundry room where Terrance was killed. Jacobson's work was noted in Hummel's supplement, but she also had her own report, Supplement #103. Although we would not receive the pictures taken by Jacobson until after we started the lawsuit in May of 2014, and would not take Jacobson's formal deposition until late 2015, our working assumption before we formally started the case in May of 2014 was that there was no blood on the MP5 based on these reports.

This was obviously significant. How could that be possible if the MP5 and its holder, Durand, were right in the middle of the melee as was alleged when Terrance was shot execution-style 10 times? If the MP5 was not in the laundry room, whose door strangely, we believed, was closed for that room at the time of the Franklin killing, then it was reasonable to conclude that Durand could not be in the room either because the MP5 never left his body due to the gun harness.

Although I am generally presenting this story in chronological order, it makes sense now to point out the deposition testimony of FS Jacobson regarding the MP5. She was deposed at the City Attorney's office in October of 2015, and like with all of the MPD personnel who were deposed, at least one lawyer for the agency was present. Jacobson was under oath as with all depositions. She had proper credentials to work in a major city's crime lab and, as of that date, she had been with MPD for 10 years. Her age was 39.

After asking her about her background, I quickly moved into her work on the Franklin case. She confirmed that she worked side-by-side with Hummel at the scene and the fact that she saw Hummel take

53

the MP5 out of Kingsbury's squad. Jacobson was right next to Hummel. I asked, "You remember seeing it, correct?"

She replied, "Correct."

After asking about the gun's condition to which she replied, "it was a big gun," I then asked, "Did you observe any blood on the gun, ma'am?"

"No. I did not."

"Did you observe any blood on it at the crime lab?"

"I did not."

"Did you test for blood in the crime lab?"

"If we don't see any visible blood, then we wouldn't test for blood."

Jacobson later confirmed under oath that she "looked all over the MP5" and that when FS Hummel took the gun out of the squad, that she "got close to it," and that there was no blood "on any portion of the gun."

Both sides of the MP5 were photographed at the crime lab. Jacobson also confirmed that to her knowledge, no GSR testing was done because MPD did not view that type of testing as "reliable."

The reality is that the Gaines' video clip caused us to dig deeper into the facts. Maybe we would have missed this MP5 evidence had Gaines' not caused us to question the official MPD version, and even in that event, we almost missed it.

Our premise was simple: If the MP5 had no blood on it, it could not have been in the laundry room when Terrance was killed – and Durand could not have been there either. With Durand accidentally discharging the gun, from what we knew from other evidence, that event of gun discharge likely would have occurred outside of the laundry room or maybe by its door – not inside. If Durand's gun had gone off accidentally, that is, Franklin had not done anything to cause the gun discharge, it seemed clear he would have been taken into custody without any problem. That is why the name, "Mookie" could be heard, we felt, on the Gaines' audio.

And then there was the strange fact that Durand handed the MP5 to his sergeant and then makes the strange comment: "It was my gun, Sarge," which was an admission, we felt, that he had accidentally fired it, shooting two of his own guys. If Terrance had actually

54

possessed the gun and shot it, one would have expected a comment from Durand to his sergeant with words to this effect: "This is the gun he grabbed, Sarge."

But why would Durand support a foolish story? When one makes up a story, it is very hard to keep all of the facts straight, and the house of cards comes falling down. Durand clearly was not responsible for executing this young black male whose only sin was attempting to evade arrest and breaking and entering, which should not have merited a death sentence. It appeared to our team that The Blue Code of Silence could be more than just silence. But if Durand had accidentally discharged his weapon shooting two of his own guys, he would have a scarlet-letter label for life and might lose his job. It sure would be nice to blame somebody else like a suspect.

The Jacobson-Hummel evidence was a wonderful revelation that gave us confidence going into the lawsuit, but we still had a lot of hard work to do including coming up with a theory, or at least a rational explanation, as to how Terrance's DNA ended up on the MP5. We would eventually address this, but we were not there yet.

Chapter Six

The Lawsuit

The Green Bay debacle was still hovering around MPD. In another January 12, 2014 story, *Strib* reporter Dave Chanen noted that Thole and Powell were appealing their December 3rd firings. Thole told Chanen the week before that both he and Powell were "assault victims" and that the MPD administration, the police union, and Green Bay officers had "betrayed them." It seemed to us they had this belief even though everyone involved had told the truth. How was the truth known? Video.

It was noted that the union was not contesting the firings, which meant that both had to pay for their own legal representation. Readers were reminded that both were full-time SWAT members. Thole's attorney felt the conduct did not justify termination. Thole had attempted to meet with Chief Harteau. She refused. He felt his firing was "politically motivated." Harteau denied this, and her denial was credible.

Thole noted he had been turned into "Lucifer" and also said, "I haven't lied about anything that happened in Green Bay... I made mistakes and was willing to take my licks. But termination? I never thought I'd have to deal with an administration that would stab me in the back." The Blue Code of Silence did not apply to the Green Bay cops. Plus, Thole could not lie even if he tried. Why? Because of the wonderful technology of video.

Before commencing suit in May of 2014, I made a decision that was perhaps the smartest for the case. The Franklin case would involve a tremendous amount of hard work and expenditure, and I felt a need for co-counsel, a lawyer teammate, to handle the case with me. I had a partner at the time, but he did not handle civil rights cases.

I approached Chicago attorney, Jay Deratany. His firm was the Deratany Law Firm, and at a later date, the firm would become

Deratany & Kosner, his partner being Mike Kosner, who would also provide a great deal of assistance to me on Franklin.

My background with Jay began in 2012. That year I was retained by a Minnesota family whose loved one, one night, had consumed a great deal of alcohol. She had given birth a few months prior, and while sleeping, accidentally rolled onto her infant son, suffocating him.

Soon thereafter, CNN's Nancy Grace show spoofed the woman on an episode, dubbing her the "Vodka Mom." Understandably, the woman had taken the death of her son very hard, but the Grace episode had put her over the edge. People began noticing the woman in public and degraded her.

Late on a July 2012 evening, she went into her sister's back yard and set herself on fire with lighter fluid. She passed away in a hospital a few days later.

Jay's firm had previously pursued CNN on a case where a Florida citizen had also committed suicide after being featured on a Nancy Grace episode. CNN challenged the case, citing the First Amendment, but eventually lost. With that precedent, and Jay's helpful input, my clients were able to promptly secure a settlement with confidential terms.

I approached Jay and Mike about Franklin. They liked the case and would become my co-counsel in August. Initially, I had the assistance of Ashwin Madia, an excellent Minnesota civil rights attorney who had graduated from New York Law School. His firm was located on the edge of downtown Minneapolis. Ashwin's firm was on the case until near the end.

The lawsuit itself, known as the "Complaint," took a long time for me to prepare. When done, it was 23 pages in length. I began the drafting it in March, but I did not finish the complaint until May. The time involved was over 100 hours to complete. We filed on May 9, 2014, and soon thereafter, served the defendants. They were Lucas Peterson, Michael Meath, Chief Harteau, and the City of Minneapolis. For cases like this, the city entity is sued, not the police agency. This is common in this type of litigation.

Civil rights cases against law enforcement for excessive force or wrongful death are normally sued out under a federal law known as the Civil Rights Act of 1983: 42 U.S.C. § 1983. It applies to illegal conduct of "state actors," which includes police officers and all members of, for example, a police agency, including the chief.

Congress presumably recognized that the truth in police excessive force cases was more likely to be figured out by plaintiffs' attorneys who would bankroll the case, which would often involve significant expenditure. This expense would be recovered in the event that a civil rights violation was proven. In addition, even if the damages were only $1.00, the defense would have to pay the attorneys' fees and costs for the plaintiff.

My introduction for the Complaint, which consisted of six paragraphs, really laid out the case. I noted in the beginning that Terrance was killed by MPD officers in an event that "need not and should not have happened - but was entirely foreseeable." I noted the "Protect and Serve with Compassion" label on MPD squads, but the reality was anything but. Their officers often engaged in excessive force with persons of color over the years. This would certainly ring true again in May of 2020 with the George Floyd matter.

I noted that those in positions of power in Minneapolis did nothing to curb the problem and would simply make large payouts as a result of civil rights claims. I delineated "a longstanding culture of disregard for the rights of young African American males who, to in-the-field MPD personnel, were considered the enemy due to a culture that bred racism to the point that racism grew to be endemic in the MPD ranks, which was especially true for MPD SWAT."

I alleged that Terrance had been successfully apprehended, clearly had surrendered, and was unarmed. He was killed in "an execution fashion due to anger and excessive force."

The factual recitation was very detailed, and we listed the specific words that could be heard on the 62-second Gaines' video clip. We did not yet know - at least at that time - of the timing of the volleys that killed Terrance, but we had: second 9: "Mookie"; second 11: "Officer shot!"; second 24: "Damn freakin' nigger"; second 27: "Man, let me go!"; second 43: "Come out little nigger!"; and second 45-46: "Don't go putting those hands up now." It was noted that 35 seconds elapsed from "officer shot" to second 46 when it was clear Terrance was still alive.

58

MPD's failure to enhance or utilize forensic testing on the Gaines' video was noted. The killing involved six rounds hitting Terrance's head, right temple, and right ear. Detail was provided alleging a botched in-house investigation. The MPD homicide investigators not implicating their own people was referenced – another version of The Blue Code of Silence. The time-gap problem was noted, the softball nature of questioning for the basement cops was pointed out, the lack of GSR testing was detailed, and in reality, anybody objectively reading this, like a federal judge, would certainly wonder if the accusations were valid. But like the old Wendy's commercial, the question would be, "Where's the beef?" We had a lot but would obtain so much more in the discovery phase. I pled various causes of action, but at the end of the day, our case was in the category of a "1983 claim" – civil rights violations. This federal law was created to address excessive force by law enforcement.

The Defendants would be required to "answer" the complaint, which they did in July with a formal document, 16 pages in length. The accusations were denied, and, as expected, the defense lawyers cited immunity, the common defense in police excessive force cases.

Susan Segal was the City Attorney at the time, but my dealings would not be with her. The senior lawyer on the case was Tim Skarda with Sara Lathrop and Brian Carter joining later. I had dealt with Tim in the past. I liked him. He fought fair and had a good sense of humor. Due to retirement, however, he would not be on the case long.

Sara and Brian were new to me. They would prove to be excellent, hardworking lawyers who would not leave a stone unturned. Both were on the case from beginning to end. Obviously, our respective theories of the case could not be more different, but this is normal in litigation. In short, they went with the basement-cop story from the original investigation and never deviated.

Around the same time that we received the answer *Strib* reporter Chanen published the fact that the city's Civil Service Commission had upheld the firings of Thole and Powell. Harteau again tried to limit the damage to those two. She said, "I didn't want people to stereotype the department for the action of others." She added: "Their firing wasn't from one single incident. They kept on with their misconduct. This is who they are." The Chief noted anti-bias training and outreach to minority communities were underway to ensure no culture of "bias" in the department. We fixated on the chief's comment: "This is who they are." So who were Stender, Peterson, Meath, Durand, and Muro? We were tasked with finding out.

After we commenced the lawsuit, there began a trail of other cases nationwide that seemed to pop up every few months. Most involved video, and the potential that members of law enforcement behaved poorly, generally resulting in the death of a black male. Michael Brown was killed in Ferguson, Missouri on August 9, 2014, which would result in protests there and nationwide and the close involvement of the Obama administration.

Our team did not have much interest in that case because early on facts came out that indicated the officer may have had just cause to end that young man's life. We were not sure. But what was more interesting to us was the killing of Eric Garner in the New York City borough of Staten Island on July 17, 2014. Unlike Brown, this one had video. However, the story took a few months to fully develop. But by December there had been over 50 demonstrations nationwide in response to it. The whole thing was depicted on citizen video. It seemed clear that Garner had been suffocated to death.

Garner again brought to the forefront for Americans the issue of use-of-force by police officers. Even people who were pro-cop including folks in Minnesota were paying attention. This type of story, completely out of our control and outside of our state, was giving our case a great boost going forward. When George Floyd was killed in Minneapolis in May of 2020, many, including me, called it Garner #2.

On October 8, 2014, we would receive more good news. Unbeknownst to us, the Department of Justice ("DOJ") was investigating MPD, perhaps as a result of the Michael Brown matter. It appeared some agencies were handpicked, including Ferguson, Missouri.

We really did not care why. What we were concerned about were the results, and the preliminary findings regarding MPD were released the day before. This was something we probably would never be able to get into evidence, but the public relations of something like this was immeasurable. This huge federal agency would not release its final report for 4-6 weeks.

Kare 11 television reporter Boua Xiong reported the main conclusion that MPD needed a better way to track officer behavior and change it "before it becomes a problem." Our interpretation of this was that the DOJ attempted to conduct an investigation, and MPD put its hands in the air and admitted they were missing competent historical data on officer behavior in the field. Whether this was true or not, the results were certainly intriguing. Chief Harteau was paying attention.

Libor Jany, another excellent reporter for the *Strib*, provided more detail about the DOJ report in his October 9 column. Chief Harteau and new Minneapolis mayor, Betsy Hodges, attended an October 8 community forum of 100 people on the same day the preliminary report was disseminated publicly. Although the column was unclear, it appeared that many of the forum attendees were people of color. At this point, the DOJ report had already received massive media coverage.

Jany attended, and Harteau said, "We're not where we want to be." Jany noted the comment was "met with sparse applause." People attending the event were apparently upset Harteau had missed the event originally scheduled for September 18 for apparently no good reason. "Before it becomes a problem". . . Wow. How that quote would resonate at the end of May of 2020.

It was our impression that folks in the Twin Cities were not buying the MPD version as to how Terrance died, even after the big September presentation by Chief Harteau. But we still had to prove our case. Now began the phase of the litigation process known as "discovery," and we had no idea going in how bizarre and fruitful that process would be.

On December 1, 2014, over four months into the litigation, Sara Lathrop sent me a letter. She asked for contact information for Jimmy Gaines. It seemed that finally, the City realized the importance of the Gaines' video clip.

Chapter Seven
The Time Gap

As of October of 2014, I had been practicing law for 28 years. I had tried over 100 cases to jury verdict, 2/3 civil, 1/3 criminal. In civil cases, the vast majority of a lawyer's time is spent on discovery, including written documents and depositions (sworn testimony under oath).

A few months went by before our opponent commenced with depositions, beginning in May of 2015. In the meantime, interrogatories (written questions), requests for documents, and request for admissions were exchanged. For us, this was really a formality since we had The 228, but we did receive five large stacks of documents from the defense attorneys, along with CD-ROMs, which included the apartment parking lot video. Other than that video, there really were no surprises except seeing the pictures of the MP5 for which no blood could be seen on the gun, confirming FS Jacobson's conclusions.

We served request for admissions on some of the defendants including Peterson. If such requests go unanswered, they are deemed admitted. We listed the words that we could hear from the Gaines' video clip. Not surprisingly, they would only admit to hearing "officer shot." Nothing else.

In April of 2015, another strange story appeared in the news regarding citizen video. On April 4, 2015, a police officer named Michael Slager killed a black man, Walter Scott, in North Charleston, South Carolina. Slager's report opined that he killed Scott because Scott had assaulted him. There was one problem for Slager: A citizen filmed the event with a camera phone, and there were huge contradictions from Slager's report version. The citizen, it appeared, on the advice of counsel, waited a few days before revealing it – which was a smart move.

The video showed Slager fire eight times at Scott as Scott was running away from him after a traffic stop. Scott was killed. Slager additionally claimed that during the scuffle, Scott tried to seize his "stun gun" as reported by the *New York Times*. The video did not support this. Also, Slager was seen planting the stun gun by Scott's dead body. Again, it was video that revealed this smoking-gun evidence. Slager was charged with murder, and demonstrations commenced nationwide. It appeared to be another really bad situation for law enforcement. The alleged grabbing of a gun by a suspect – a convenient excuse. That sounded familiar to us.

I coordinated depositions with Sara Lathrop. We knew depositions, especially of the basement SWAT team, would be important for prevailing in the case. MPD's history with 1983 civil rights death cases was to always move for summary judgment based on immunity. This would be a motion where the defense alleges the case should be dismissed, and as such, if granted, there would be no jury trial. The key for us was to generate evidence to convince the federal judge, in this case, Donovan Frank, that there were fact issues appropriate for a jury. The defense would then have to deal with the pros and cons of proceeding to trial rather than settling. If we could generate evidence that Terrance was murdered, Judge Frank would deny the defendants' motion. It was that simple. But we knew no matter what our evidence was, the defendants would likely proceed with that motion. We were already getting the vibe that they would basically be ignoring the evidence from the Gaines' video clip. But we also had a feeling that they would likely be tone-deaf with evidence such as the lack of any blood on the MP5 as the Jacobson and Hummel supplements revealed.

It was decided that Sara's office would begin with depositions in May, which would be of Walt Franklin, Terrance's half siblings, and a couple of witnesses from the bike shop. We felt the need to promptly deal with the key time-gap witness, Metro Transit cop Geoffrey Wyatt, the one who said "officer shot" in front of the Bickal home. This meant I would be dealing with another agency and at least one other lawyer other than those for defense counsel.

Before we proceeded with the depositions, like clockwork, another national story evolved regarding the death of a black male. It

63

would be yet another questionable death of a citizen in custody of law enforcement. The venue this time was Baltimore, Maryland, a place I had been to often in my youth mostly for pro sporting events.

The victim this time was named Freddie Gray. He was arrested on April 12, 2015 and died on April 19, 2015, allegedly due to injuries to his spinal cord. The facts were somewhat convoluted, but it appeared Gray was injured in police custody, and there was video to indicate he basically was treated like garbage. The case resulted in many massive protests in the Baltimore area and then nationwide. The officers in question would eventually be charged. The city would issue a large payout to Gray's heirs.

What typically would happen with cases like this, and we were reaping the benefit, was that media would go down tributaries of topics such as with use-of-force statistics. For example, a *New York Times* story by Michael Wines and Sarah Cohen noted that use of police force against minorities – and whites too – was not tracked well. The lead in their May 1, 2015 story read: "The use of police force . . . is so poorly monitored that there is no precise accounting of how many citizens are killed by officers, much less their ethnicity or other crucial details." The story went on to note that for years, FBI data on so called "justifiable police homicides" had understated the problem.

The first deposition of substance before Wyatt was Jimmy Gaines. Defense counsel understood the Gaines' video clip could no longer be ignored, and Jimmy appeared at their office on May 20, 2015. He was subpoenaed but would have willingly cooperated anyway. Sara handled the deposition for the defense. I attended for our team.

Jimmy brought with him the iPod Touch he used on May 1, along with a flash drive. It was provided directly to an expert defense counsel had retained for the sound issue who was present at the deposition.

Jimmy described his strange experience on May 10, 2013 as a "bad day where everyone lost." When he recorded the video that day, something for which he had prior professional experience, he was more concentrated on "getting the video shot" than listening.

Sara asked him what words he could hear off the video clip, which he replied was only "officer shot," but he readily admitted that he had a hearing problem. Really, all he heard after "officer shot" was

64

shouting. He never attempted enhancement of the audio on his own because of his hearing issues. He noted hearing the "small boom" and the "large boom" but could not recall any other detail. He admitted that he had trouble recalling the sequence of events. The energy in the air was palpable. All police he saw had guns drawn.

The device was returned to him before he left, and he noted that this deposition was the first time he had done anything "formal" for this event. The police had never contacted him, and he had never given a statement at their request. To us, it was as if MPD preferred that Jimmy not exist.

Sara took Jim Bickal's deposition the same day. There was a problem that came up that had to be addressed promptly. Jim testified for the most part consistent with his statement as was disclosed back in Chapter 1. But he said he heard "one set of shots" and "one flurry of activity."

This of course would be a huge problem for Walt's case because, as the Plaintiff, we were trying to prove that there was a significant time gap between the time the officers were shot and the time that Terrance was killed, which would be strong circumstantial evidence to prove that Terrance was murdered – supported by the Gaines' video.

In a deposition, like at trial, the other attorney who did not serve notice of the deposition is also allowed to ask questions. Normally, how a lawyer asks questions in a discovery deposition is typically more open ended than in a trial in front of a jury. But since Jim said something that could really hurt our case, I had to address it right away in a format known as cross-examination. This would be easy. I referred Jim to his Q&A taken on June 18, 2013 by Porras, Supplement #107.

I established with Jim that his memory would have been better then than it is now, almost two years later. I then confirmed his knowledge that the north side door was obviously open, an important fact for us, when he saw an injured officer being carried out that door. The window he was looking out of in a southerly direction, toward that door, was closed, which presumably would have affected his ability to hear sounds outside.

I then asked Jim to look at Exhibit 1, his statement: "About two-thirds of the way down, there is a question that says, and let me know if you find this, 'Okay, and um when the officers went in . . .' Do you see that?"

"Yes."

"And it then says, 'When the officers went in, did you hear anything? Did you hear any shots being fired?' And your answer was, 'No. I didn't hear the shots being fired.'"

"Yep."

"Is it possible, Sir, that the notion that there may have been shots fired was something that you observed from your neighbor reacting to something?"

"Yes."

The problem had been immediately neutralized from MPD's own report. This also illustrated that when a witness misstates something, they can sometimes make a mistake – or just get crossed up. Perhaps that is the origin of the term "cross-examination." Jim had just made a mistake and did not recall correctly.

I had gotten to know Jim fairly well since I was retained. He was really angry at the police for what had happened in his home, and although he never had told me specifically that he did not buy the official police version, I had gotten that distinct impression. Jim felt bad for Terrance's family, but he certainly was not someone who would lie under oath for any reason. In my experience, most people fall into that category. It was unfortunate that Terrance had chosen his home, but Jim was not angry about the strange set of circumstances that literally ended up on his doorstep. Jim was a good, solid citizen.

It was now time for Geoffrey Wyatt's deposition. I had waited for this moment with baited breath since I had first realized the significance of "officer shot" when both of us, my investigator Steve Rogers and I, determined the Gaines' video clip content.

Jimmy had recorded six video clips that day. From an earlier clip, Wyatt, who was working in his capacity with Metro Transit Police, was right in front of the Bickal home. It seemed he was merely covering that spot in case the suspect came out that way. This person, who appeared to us to be Wyatt, had a gun out pointed right at the front door.

66

There were time elements we concentrated on such as the fact Wyatt clearly had learned that an officer had been shot before he verbalized "officer shot." It seemed reasonable to assume that when he found that out, he would have probably run from that spot to the side of the house and then back, and it was the trip back where he made that statement. Steve and I were so fixated on this concept that we went to the Bickal home and made the run ourselves to see how long it took us. Each direction was about five seconds.

Therefore, we had these questions we needed answers to for the time element:

1. Did Wyatt move right away upon hearing a cop had been shot?
2. How long did it take Wyatt to get from the front of the house to his first chosen destination?
3. How long did he stay there?
4. When he decided to move from there to the spot where he said "officer shot," how much time elapsed?

We were working with a gap already of 35 seconds from second 11: "Officer shot" to the last voice directive at second 46 on the Gaines' clip. We obviously wanted a larger gap but not too large because it would come off as too conspiratorial. Peterson and Meath had to do their dirty deed quickly to get away with it. To involve other officers, especially those outside of the SWAT team, would be too risky for them.

Our gap goal was 60 seconds, maybe 90 seconds at most. We felt the killing of Terrance was not premeditated. It was a knee jerk reaction, we felt, from the notion in the cops' minds that Terrance had tried to run over a cop. The mess that happened in the basement with the accidental discharge was such that they promptly blamed Terrance for that situation also. It was like a line from a movie. In their minds, Terrance "needed" killing.

I took Wyatt's deposition at the MTC main office in downtown St. Paul. Tim Skarda appeared for the defense. There was no question in my mind that Wyatt's attorney had been closely briefed about the time gap and, as such, Wyatt would now know the significance about why he was so important.

Although I felt for the most part that Wyatt was honest, he knew all law-enforcement eyes were on him, and I felt he hedged a bit. But I did catch him in a little, let us say, confusion, about a fact before he heard that an officer had been shot. He admitted to me his gun was out, but he alleged he was not pointing it at anything. But when I showed him the Gaines' clip that depicted him in front of the Bickal house, one could clearly see that Wyatt was in fact pointing it. I asked, "So what you were doing after you arrived was ... you were guarding the perimeter. You had your gun drawn. And would you agree you were pointing it at the front door?"

"I appeared to be pointing it at something. I don't know what I would be pointing it at."

This would be a matter for the jury to decide, but it was an important admission that he was pointing his gun bolstering the fact that the situation was very intense as articulated by people like Bickal neighbor Anthony Oberlander from the beginning. This was a small point, but small points combined together win cases. The bottom line is that it was obvious that Wyatt never would have admitted that in a million years but for the technology of video.

I then moved on to the questions of timing. The atmosphere in the deposition was tense. Usually, discovery depositions can be fairly mundane. That would not be true for this case, at least for the depositions we scheduled. It seemed like every deposition was tense, and Wyatt's was no exception.

Tim Skarda was a smart lawyer. He was prepared and knew exactly where I was going. But there was not much he could do besides give Wyatt's lawyer a heads up as to why Wyatt's testimony was so significant. Whether Tim did that or not, we did not know, but this witness was not his client.

Wyatt agreed understandably that his memory about these facts would have been better when he prepared his report rather than now, over two years later. His report had the heading "Metro Transit Police Department-Incident Report." The five-page report was prepared at 18:38 on the date of the incident, or 6:38 p.m. Of course, the timing questions I was about to ask him were not addressed in his report. Now here he was, over two years later, dealing with an inquisitive attorney in a high-profile case. This increased the intensity. Wyatt admitted that the report did refresh his memory, which is one of the reasons that reports of any kind even exist. Nobody could criticize that answer.

Wyatt was monitoring police radio traffic on May 10, 2013 when he heard there was a suspect in flight. He came to the scene because he was not far away. He was training an officer named Chad DeGree that day, an officer who had plenty of experience with the St. Paul Police Department. Wyatt recalled that he was the first member of law enforcement to arrive in a squad in front of the Bickal house. DeGree deployed on the northwest side, and Wyatt confirmed his location in the front of the home or on the west side. Less than five minutes after they arrived, Wyatt heard the message from his shoulder mic, in a panicked voice, "We have an officer shot."

Wyatt's response was to run to the left or the north side of the house. Facing the house, he would have been looking to the east. When he arrived on the north side, he saw the door at that location was open, which was another important fact for us to establish.

I asked Wyatt to give me a time frame for his spot to that side door. All I could get out of him was "moments." He stated that by this he meant seconds, but he refused to give a specific time estimate. I was okay with this. Perhaps he would later give an estimate. We were just beginning the whole time concept.

Wyatt then entered the door and saw a commotion at the bottom of the basement steps. He then saw an officer being carried up. It seemed clear to us his arrival was probably right at the time that Officer Gorman had just opened the door.

I asked Wyatt about hearing gunshots. Other than saying he heard gun shots, he could not say how many or anything about sequence or any cadence between shots. It was hard to say if he was being truthful about this or was just confused. He did concede that he had "no idea" as to when Terrance was killed.

Someone – he did not recall who – asked for a tourniquet. I then asked him this big question: "After you got to that door, how long were you at that spot before you went to get your first aid kit?"

"Just guessing on time, I would say less than 20 seconds."

I was okay with that. We were hopeful for that, not much more. He then admitted that the tourniquet request caused him to move right away, a not surprising reaction. His mindset then was to move toward his vehicle. Another big question: "How long did it take you to get to your vehicle from the point you were at?"

"I guess however long it took for me to run from the door to my squad that was parked in front of the house. Less than ten seconds." Wyatt had now just given an estimate for an initial movement from the front of the house to the north side of the house because it was the same route.

Other questions were asked, but we had reached our goal. Although his testimony was not specifically concrete, we were hopeful for an additional 30 seconds, and in the grand scheme of things, his time estimates seemed reasonable. Based on our investigation, and Steve and I running around the outside of the Bickal home like chickens with our heads cut off, we felt a time estimate of five seconds from front door to side door was reasonable. Then to get the first aid kit up to the "officer shot" spot was another five seconds. When one added the roughly 20-second prediction for how long he was at the north side door, a reasonable time estimate, we now had the time gap at about 65 seconds - the original 35 seconds, 46 minus 11, and then another 30 seconds from Wyatt.

How significant was this gap? If the fact-finding jury believed it, this evidence alone meant it was likely that Terrance Franklin had been murdered, and the MPD version as to how things went down was entirely made up. But we still had a problem. Why could we not hear the gunshot volleys that killed Terrance? They should have been picked up by the Gaines' device, and the fact that they had possibly not been picked up potentially cut against the credibility of that evidence.

Also, to have a concrete line of demarcation as to when Terrance was specifically killed could be extremely helpful. We hoped it was an achievable goal. We would soon find out, and it was a matter of finding a really smart guy.

In a civil case like ours, the litigants have the ability to retain experts for technical matters that can assist the jury with their fact-finding duties. We felt that we needed five experts. We did repeatedly consult with a DNA expert as explained herein, but we ended up officially with four: Richard Ernest from Texas, firearms' incident reconstructionist; Charles Drago from Florida, a former police chief for police excessive force issues; Sean Harrington, a local expert regarding "metadata" – authenticating the Gaines' video clip timing wise with police radio evidence; and Ed Primeau from Michigan for audio/sound technical issues. All of these men were brilliant in their fields, and their addition to our already current team of my staff, co-counsel - Jay, Mike, and Ashwin - and Steve Rogers, resulted in a formidable team. Later, Alan Rogers from Tennessee would join us as a firearms' consultant.

As time went on, I developed a strong friendship with Ed Primeau. He was also a music junkie like me and had actually produced an interesting documentary on Bob Seger, a Detroit icon. Ed was recognized as one of the top audio experts in the nation. His resume was off-the-chart impressive. Ed was a sound junkie. It was amazing to us how a concept like sound could be so complicated.

Ed could certainly do audio enhancement, and we wanted his input as to what he could hear on the main Gaines' video clip, but his opinions in this regard probably would not get into evidence because that would "invade the province of the jury." What could be heard was their job, not Ed's. But we needed to provide a rational, scientific explanation as to how the Gaines' device was able to pick up sounds and words from the basement. We also hoped he could solve the mystery as to why we could not hear or locate the gunshots that killed Terrance. We were confident the original discharge of the MP5 was a timeframe just before Jimmy started recording so that could not be heard. But what about the shots that killed Terrance? They should be on there.

We retained Ed in June of 2015, and soon thereafter, he had the six Gaines' video clips. The plan was for me to complete the depositions of Wyatt and DeGree, go see him at his sound studio in Rochester Hills, and then develop a plan for scene investigation outside of and hopefully inside the Bickal home. Ed's son Michael would be a tremendous asset to Ed's team.

After completing Wyatt's deposition on June 30, 2015, I had planned to be in Ed's sound studio by July 7th. It should be noted that I deposed Chad DeGree right after Wyatt. DeGree, who was near the home like Wyatt, alleged he heard two shots then a gap involving yelling with a time frame of 10-15 seconds when he then heard another series of shots. There were two problems with his recollection: The

Gaines' video, juxtaposed with Wyatt's testimony, was now a much better source for the time gap, and the other problem was that DeGree's time-gap estimate was not in his report. As such, it was unlikely that any reasonable juror would believe his gap estimate to be credible. Although the fact that DeGree even articulated a gap was interesting. Terrance should have been killed immediately after an officer was shot. Even 10 to 15 seconds was arguably problematic for the defendants.

My visit to Ed's studio was a day I will never forget. It is right up there with the birth of my son. The hope was that with the clarity of the studio maybe I would hear something that I had not already heard, but I did not have any grandiose notions. I just felt it was something I had to do to not leave any stone unturned.

With Ed and Mike assisting, I was able to hear the key words we already had, just more clearly. The main clip was 62 seconds in length. For the longest time, the last thing we could hear of any significance was the end of "don't go putting those hands up now," which ended at second 46 of the clip. But then, miraculously, starting at second 53, I heard sounds that I would describe as "booms," which extended for several seconds. I heard six. Ed and Mike pointed them out to me. This made sense because even though there were more than six shots, the sequence of the shots was such that it was reasonable to assume some of the rounds fired by Peterson and Meath were simultaneous. Peterson had already agreed to this in his Q&A.

It was unbelievable. We could now hear the shots that killed Terrance! Part of the problem was that there was a jet flying overhead that affected the clarity of hearing the shots, but both Ed and Mike felt they were gunshots, and eventually, our police expert, Chuck Drago, said there was no question in his mind that they were gunshots. In addition, the gunshot sounds were coming from a small interior room of the basement with a door that was probably closed so the sounds were presumably muffled. But this would be a decision for the jury, not our experts. However, they sure sounded like a gun or guns going off.

Now that we had a specific line of demarcation as to when Terrance was killed, we had these reasonable conclusions based on the words that could be heard on the key Gaines' video clip:

72

1. "Mookie." 28 seconds after an officer was shot.
2. "Officer shot!" (by Wyatt). 30 seconds after.
3. "Damn freakin' nigger." 45 seconds after.
4. "Man, let me go." 46 seconds after.
5. "Come out little nigger." 62 seconds after.
6. "Don't go putting those hands up now." 64 seconds after.
7. The gunshots – 6 shots. 72 seconds after.

The 30-second additional time estimate based on Wyatt's testimony could certainly be adjusted give or take 5-10 seconds, but either way, a time gap of 60-70 seconds from the time an officer was shot to the killing of Terrance was an excellent fact for what we were trying to prove.

Based on the sound-lab revelations, it was obvious Ed and Mike had to come to the Bickal home so that Ed could eventually explain to a jury how it was that this simple iPod Touch device could pick up sounds from the basement. Ed would have to see the physical configuration of the landscape by the Bickal home to figure this out. Ed had already deduced in his lab that the source of the sounds did not come out of an open shoulder mic. Ed described this as a sound concept known as "slap delay." It was Ed's quick deduction that the Gaines' device picked up sounds emanating directly out of the basement through the open north side door, but he would have to confirm this with field investigation.

In early August, Ed came with his team to the Twin Cities, and we were able to access the porch that Jimmy filmed from along with the Bickal basement. We gave our opponent a heads up in the event that they wished to observe what we were doing. The process was quite interesting. To actually access the Bickal basement myself where the whole thing went down was pretty eerie. I was surprised at how small the basement was, including the laundry room, the place where I was confident my client's son, Terrance, had been executed. The home was something like 100 years old as I recall. Jimmy Gaines actually came by also, and Ed and Mike had a chance to speak with him.

Ed's technical expertise completely confirmed his hypothesis that the words picked up by the Gaines' device, at least those most

73

critical to our case, did emanate directly out of the basement to be memorialized by the device forever. Ed described it to me in this way: Because the basement was so small, it created a situation that what happened, from an audio perspective, allowed the sound to come easily out the north side door. In other words, had that door not been open, those key words, picked up after an officer had been shot and that door was opened, never would have been recorded.

Ed referred to a "compartmentalized small area with reflective surfaces" such that there was no space to absorb the voices and, therefore, the voices and other sounds carried "far out." Ed told me that to be there and to hear other sounds like airplanes, cars, etcetera, he could experience in person the sound reflections off of the house, which was extremely valuable to his perception. This particular neighborhood, as Ed explained, was an "acoustic chamber" meaning that physical objects being close together and very old caused the sounds to be "very reflective," which means that sound can "bounce and easily travel."

Earlier in the day, we had gone to a gun range and performed sound testing comparing live rounds to blanks. The decibel levels were almost identical. Ed would eventually prepare his final report in October.

The time frame of about a month from June 30 to early August had allowed us to achieve one of our goals – confirming the time gap with evidence and science. We had no doubt that Judge Frank would consider this evidence when addressing the defendants' inevitable immunity motion. We next had to deal with the DNA evidence that had been hanging over us like a black cloud. That was coming up, and soon.

Chapter Eight
A Mystery is Solved

We knew going into litigation that possibly our toughest challenge was addressing the contention that Terrance's DNA was on the MP5 when analyzed after the incident. The DNA match was determined by the Minnesota Bureau of Criminal Apprehension, known as the "BCA." This was an agency none of our team trusted, but their workup on the DNA seemed credible. Historically, when investigating claims of excessive force against Minnesota law enforcement agencies, the BCA had never rendered a decision against any of those entities. In the later Justine Damond matter they would be universally criticized for doing a poor job.

From the beginning, our DNA consultant felt that the close quarters in the laundry room with blood spray and just the whole circumstance was important. Based on the initial beating of Terrance and Terrance being shot multiple times, the notion that "touch DNA" could be on the MP5 was not surprising.

We were told that touch DNA was comparable to trace DNA, which would only require a very small sample for a positive test. But we wanted something more than just a vague contention that the close quarters of the basement could explain the DNA match for Terrance. There were other scenarios too. If Terrance had been standing and was knocked to the ground by what was clearly a vicious assault and an attack by K-9 Nash, he could have inadvertently touched the MP5 to break his fall. The point is there could be numerous scenarios, innocent explanations, as to how his DNA ended up on the gun. Considering the large time gap and the other evidence to support murder, the DNA issue was arguably a minor matter, but we could not ignore it. It had to be dealt with. Fortunately, it would be solved with only one discovery deposition.

Dave Schiebel, DOC Dave, was a combo platter-type witness. He was involved with the initial apprehension with Smulski and

Moore. The detail for this will be addressed in the next chapter, but he also ended up in the basement after Terrance had been killed. Our team at times would think about the strange supplement of Officer Timothy Gorman who went into the Bickal basement after the two injured officers had been removed. He checked for signs of life then saw DOC Dave was down there with the body, strangely, alone. We were not sure what that meant. It was a bizarre fact that raised our antennas.

DOC Dave would be our next deposition of substance. Our investigation revealed that Dave was someone who located fugitives for the DOC, and he was particularly close to MPD, almost like he was an employee of that agency. When he was subpoenaed at his private home for trial in 2019 (he had retired since 2013), he was actually wearing a shirt with an "MPD" label on it.

We were always intrigued by Dave's Supplement #48, in The 228. After Terrance was killed, Dave was in the basement with the other SWAT cops, and he referenced a "Minneapolis Officer" handing him the MP5. We assumed this was Durand, but Dave's report was vague as to this officer's identity. Now we finally would be able to get detail – under oath.

We deposed him at our office on August 12, 2015. He was represented by an attorney with the Minnesota Attorney General's Office. When I questioned him, he was just about to turn 60. His work for the DOC had him assigned with the U.S. Marshals Service with a direct connection to MPD. For a peace officer, he was particularly short, under 5'5" tall. Overall, he had an unassuming presence. He was incredibly nervous for his deposition, perhaps more nervous than any witness I had ever deposed. He testified that his association to MPD had been for 20 years. That was the close link we had expected.

On May 10, 2013, when he was away from his squad, he had a clip-on Motorola radio device on his person so he could monitor police radio traffic. Just before the SWAT team went into the Bickal home, Dave was positioned outside on the northeast corner of the Bickal home. After the events at the apartment complex (the beginning of the event), he then assisted other officers to find Terrance by searching other homes in the neighborhood.

At about 3:30 p.m., Dave heard "numerous shots" from inside the home. He claimed he then opened the "north side door" of the home with an officer he described as the "MTC officer," which we presumed had to be Wyatt. Just then, Stender was coming out and advised that an officer had been shot. We were reasonably confident, at this point, Terrance had yet to be killed.

At some later point, after officers had cleared out of the basement, Dave admitted that he ended up in the laundry room where Terrance's dead body was. He attempted to determine if Terrance was dead by feeling with his fingers on Terrance's neck and wrist. When Dave did this, he believed that he was alone in the room with the decedent. After the vital-sign check, he claimed he remained in the basement for "less than 5 minutes." Nobody at the scene told Dave how the two MPD officers ended up shot.

In terms of the number of shots that Dave had heard, his testimony was vague. When asked about this topic, he said, "I heard a series of shots...it was more than one shot. It was multiple shots, but I couldn't tell you how many." Dave typed up his own statement at 20:33, just after 8:30 p.m. that evening.

It seemed clear to me that Dave knew the primary reason why I was taking his deposition, and he had been closely coached. It was almost as if he was a party to the case – a sued defendant.

Amazingly, after Dave checked for signs of life on the dead suspect, he admitted, corroborating his report, that an MPD officer had given him the MP5. The mystery as to who that was was now solved.

Q. At some point, a gun was handed to you, correct?
A. Correct.

...

A. . . .And it was at that time Durand, who was one of the SWAT guys, was going to assist them. And he said, "Dave, I am going to give you my MP5."

This was incredible evidence and provided a perfectly innocent explanation as to how Terrance's DNA ended up on that gun. Dave touched Terrance's body and then the gun Terrance allegedly used to shoot the two officers was given directly to Dave! Chief Harteau conveniently failed to tell the public about this at her highly publicized press conference in September of 2013. Since her presser was right after the grand jury had determined not to indict, it seemed obvious that this evidence was not presented, and that the whole process was a whitewash including the fact Jimmy Gaines did not testify.

But it got even better – the type of evidence in a case like this that was of the smoking-gun variety.

> Q. He [Durand] knew you on a first name basis, correct?
> A. I believe so, yeah.
> Q. And you knew him on a first name basis?
> A. No. I did not.
> Q. But the point is someone handed you an MP5?
> A. Correct…And he said something to me, which at the time didn't make any sense. I believe what he said was: "This is the gun that caused the injuries." So I am under the assumption that this is the gun that they shot the deceased with.

So we now had two strange comments by Durand: He told Sergeant Strauss right after that, "It was my gun, Sarge"; then to Dave, also right after: "This is the gun that caused the injuries." This is exactly what an officer might say in a case of accidental discharge assuaging one's guilt by blaming the gun and not yourself, as the handler of the gun. Importantly, it was two golden opportunities early for Durand to make clear to two separate people that it was the suspect who caused the gun to discharge, that is, intentionally shot the gun. Durand did not do that. This was the type of evidence that was arguably even better than the now reasonable explanation for the DNA evidence.

But DOC Dave thought he could outsmart us. He provided an elaborate explanation that when the MP5 was given to him, it was put over his shoulder with the strap. His point was he did not touch it. In light of the chaotic situation in the basement with injured officers, the notion that the gun was handed to him in that fashion was not credible, and certainly my assumption right away was that no juror would believe that. This description was not in his report. But Dave had another trick up his sleeve. He claimed that when he went down into the basement, he actually put gloves on before he touched Terrance's body checking for vitals, although he later made clear that his fingers did not touch any blood.

There were several problems with this glove scenario as this portion of the Schiebel deposition revealed:

Q. And is it your testimony that before you attempted to ascertain if he had a pulse, you put gloves on?
A. Correct.
Q. Where were your gloves? On your person?
A. On my person.

Dave then described the type of glove and was then asked if he had referenced the gloves in his report. He said he could not recall. I did not refresh his memory with the report that in fact he had not, but rather, moved to another area of inquiry.

Q. Were those gloves ever secured as evidence by MPD?
A. Negative.
Q. Where are the gloves?
A. I threw them away.

He then alleged that he took the gloves off and stuck them in his pocket, but he added that he did not believe that there was any blood on the gloves. So the man known affectionately as DOC Dave had presumably touched the MP5, left nothing visible such as blood, and had no evidence of substance to support his contention that he wore gloves for this process. He failed to reference them in his report, failed to keep them, and nobody at the scene could vouch for the notion that he had gloves on when he touched Terrance's body - and when he was later handed the MP5.

We had another reason to support our belief that Dave had been completely dishonest about the gloves. He did not think this through, and if anyone had advised him to come up with the glove story, they additionally had not thought it through. Here was the problem for DOC Dave and the defendants as a whole: The BCA analysis determined that the DNA of one, Dave Schiebel, aka DOC Dave, was on the MP5 in multiple places. The reasonable conclusion therefore was that Dave had lied about the gloves. But I did not nail him with this evidence in his deposition. I would wait for trial for that.

When I briefed our DNA consultant on these facts, he said, "Mike, it looks like you don't even need me now. Lay people will understand this without a DNA expert."

The DNA problem, which had been on the forefront of our brains since August of 2013, leaked by MPD personnel in a sleazy way, was now solved three days before the two-year anniversary of us finding out about it. And neither Chief Harteau nor her two homicide investigators had ever mentioned one syllable to the public about the DOC Dave evidence back in 2013.

Chapter Nine

The Apartment Video

Discovery so far had been fruitful. We had developed excellent additional evidence to support our time-gap theory, we had neutralized the DNA problem, and we had discovered strong evidence to support the contention that Durand was not in the laundry room when Peterson and Meath massacred Terrance. This would later be confirmed with the deposition of FS Jacobson near the end of discovery.

The purpose of deposing the SWAT basement team would be to neutralize them or perhaps develop new evidence to help our working theories and also, to generate evidence to defeat the inevitable defense summary judgment motion. Considering how preposterous their stories were in light of other evidence, it seemed clear to us that they would not fare well under oath. But that remained to be seen.

In the meantime, there was another issue we had to address: the initial attempted apprehension. There seemed to always be this vague accusation that Terrance had attempted to run over a police officer in the initial attempt to apprehend him, but Sergeant Katherine Smulski did not allege that in her report. What would she say about that under oath?

Cala Scott had told us from the beginning that an older female officer had walked up to her at the scene and said Terrance "had tried to kill her." Our belief as a team was that this was Smulski, and if Smulski said that to a bystander or potential witness, what was she telling fellow cops in the field? And if it went out over the cop radio airwaves, there was no telling how many MPD personnel had heard it. Muro said he heard it, or words to that effect. We definitely felt Peterson heard it or knew it from others, and if he did, his mindset may have been that Terrance was an attempted cop killer. This would be further incentive for Peterson to have murdered Terrance.

After we received the defendants' disclosures, we finally were able to see the video from the Lyndale Avenue apartment where the police first attempted apprehension of Terrance. He backed Cala's car out and drove off. The notion he tried to run a cop over was not supported by the video images at all. Steve Rogers agreed with me. Had Chief Harteau seen this? In fact, it even looked like Smulski had kicked the car as Terrance drove by. She did not seem scared. The facts seemed to be to the contrary. But what did Smulski tell others in the field? Had she exaggerated? And what was the position of Sergeant Moore and DOC Dave on this issue? They were right there when it happened.

When Cala got her car back, she saw that there was a hole in the front bumper, which was a sample MPD had carved out for testing. There was no apology, and no attempt by MPD to compensate her for the damage. What did the damage consist of from Terrance's driving conduct? A report confirmed that there was a small amount of paint transfer that could hardly be seen. There was no property damage at all that would require a body shop. But that was not the apparent mindset of MPD personnel when they were searching for Terrance on the afternoon of May 10, 2013. We believed they thought he had tried to run over Smulski.

We were angry. If Chief Harteau was truly being transparent, she should have shown the public the apartment video at the September 2013 presser when she told the public her officers had done nothing wrong in the basement of the Bickal home.

My impression of Chief Harteau was that she was a person of integrity committed to fixing what she knew was an agency with major-league problems. How did she get dragged into this thing and support a false narrative? Had she seen the evidence? Had the homicide investigators scammed her from seeing the truth, intentionally or otherwise? The bottom line was that by supporting the false narrative, she was right in the mix with The Blue Code of Silence.

I deposed Smulski on October 2, 2015 and, like all other MPD personnel, this took place at the City Attorney's Office. I had already deposed Sergeant Gerald Moore and DOC Dave, the substance of which I will note later in this chapter. Smulski had been on the force for 28 years, was 51 years old, and had just retired in May. Caucasian, she was a tough looking woman, tougher I felt than many of the male officers of MPD.

She was a confrontational witness, perhaps more than any other officer in the case, including the SWAT basement team. My primary purpose with her deposition was to prove she had overstated the events at the Lyndale apartment parking lot and that Terrance had merely driven away. It was clear that Terrance did not want to be apprehended. From the beginning of the case, we had heard that he had a warrant, and he did not want to be in jail for his son's birthday, which was coming up soon. Young people, especially males, can run for the dumbest reasons. Even possession of a small amount of marijuana, a petty misdemeanor, can sometimes cause a young male to run. But the more important question was whether Terrance had tried to run over Smulski and, more importantly, whether that was true or not, if Smulski conveyed that message to other cops in the field.

I had seen in other cases that there could be a tendency for police personnel to exaggerate events in the field, especially in the middle of a full-blown cover-up. It was a little hard to predict her testimony on the key issues even though I had her supplement.

The Smulski deposition would not be long, but I would secure helpful evidence especially compared to other testimony. We really had Smulski, Moore, and DOC Dave in a big disadvantage because of the apartment video. In short, we could see what happened, but there was no audio. Video was changing the world in terms of citizen perception of police conduct, and that was certainly true with the two key videos we had in the Franklin case. Both were tremendously helpful.

Smulski stated that she reviewed her report, Supplement #468, in advance of her deposition. She also admitted watching the Gaines' video. She claimed that not only could she not hear any words at all, she could not even hear voices. This was strange since it seemed everyone could at least hear "officer shot." She literally was claiming that she could not hear anything in terms of words.

Smulski had seen the apartment video before her grand jury testimony but not before she prepared her supplement at 21:30, or 9:30 pm, on the date of the incident. She understandably admitted that her memory was better when she prepared the supplement rather than today - almost 2 ½ years later. She additionally claimed that the apartment video confirmed the accuracy of her report.

She went to the Lyndale apartment complex aware that the 911 call concerned a person who may have previously committed a burglary there. It was not an active burglary. There was no information the person was armed. She arrived around the same time as Moore and DOC Dave.

The driver of the PT Cruiser, Terrance, was given verbal commands. She also used the PA on her squad. She saw that the driver put the car in reverse, and her reaction was to get out of her vehicle because he was not complying. She described the back up as "slow." He drove toward her. She claimed that she had to move out of the way, or she would be hit. She further alleged that the driver struck a door of her squad as he left the parking lot. This caused the door to shut. But did she really have to move out of the way? The video would be the best source.

She confirmed the hit on the door caused a simple transfer of paint, no dent. She then said she did not jump out of the way, but rather, "walked fastly." Her belief then was that Terrance was trying to injure or kill her.

This is where things became strange. She testified that she told others in the field Terrance had tried to injure or kill her, but she admitted after reading her report that she did not note that belief or contention in her report. If that was the case, it would seem reasonable that would be the main point the reporting officer would make. But she then claimed that she did not radio this fact to others in the field.

Q. So it was your belief at the time, your perception, he was trying to injure or kill you, correct?

A. Yes.

. . .

Q. Did you put that in your report?

A. Put what?

Q. That he was trying to kill or injure you?

84

A. If it is not in there, I don't know. I have to read it again. I don't know.

Q. Again, this is Supplement 55 from page 53 of the 234-page report. You can read it and tell me if it is in there, please. [Witness given time to read.] Is it in there, ma'am?

A. Not in those words, no.

Q. Did you at some point radio that to others – what happened to you?

A. I did not, no.

This was bizarre. If a suspect had attempted to injure or kill her, it would seem to be a knee-jerk reaction for any cop to let others in the field know that. She then claimed Moore was the one who radioed that the suspect tried to injure or kill her. She noted that she said this to MPD personnel in the field in person but not by radio. She could not give an estimate as to how many officers she said this to, and she could not provide any names of the recipients of this message. Her explanation for not detailing this in the report was that the notion the suspect tried to injure or kill her would be "an opinion" not "a fact." After Terrance left, she accidentally pursued another vehicle that ended up not being his.

She later was at the perimeter on 27th between Bryant and Colfax. At that spot, she was with another officer and "possibly" told this person detail about what happened at the apartment complex parking lot.

At some point later that day, she spoke with Moore about what happened. She "may have" discussed the facts with Moore, but she could not say when. She was unsure if it was before or after she heard "officer shot" coming out of another officer's shoulder mic or from a squad radio.

I showed her a report of a Lieutenant Diaz that noted the "suspect vehicle nearly struck Sergeant Smulski hitting her fully marked squad." Diaz had met with her and Moore. Smulski claimed that this did not refresh her memory as to what she told Diaz. She

85

further testified that she had been trained on being accurate in reports and not to exaggerate. I then asked her about Cala Scott. She admitted speaking with Cala at the scene before she became aware that Terrance had been killed. I did not think she would admit to what she told Cala, but I asked anyway: "Did you say to her words to the effect of he, meaning Terrance Franklin, tried to kill you? Did you say something like that to her?"

"I don't recall saying that, no."

"Is it possible you may have said that? You just don't remember?"

"I don't remember."

The deposition had served its purpose. The video had shown clearly a person trying to exit the parking lot but not trying to kill anyone. And Smulski said nothing in her report about Terrance trying to kill her because that was the truth. But it was equally obvious that she was telling anyone who would listen in the field it was her belief the suspect tried to kill her. That message would spread like wildfire regardless. In conclusion, we objectively felt that she was a poor witness who not only hurt the defense, but provided evidence supporting our theories.

Sergeant Moore's deposition would be additionally helpful. Moore would be the only MPD witness who I would depose in the entire case who was African American. He had been on the force for 30 years and was 61 years old when I deposed him on September 30, 2015.

I felt bad for Moore. He was someone who revealed humanity and, at one point, he almost cried in the deposition. I felt he knew the truth and wanted to help the Franklin family, but the strong grip of The Blue Code had him. Once it had a member of law enforcement in its clutches, it was like an eagle holding onto a trout. That fish would not escape. The Blue Code of Silence was an evil entity, more evil than we had imagined at the time we commenced the lawsuit.

Other than submitting his report and securing DOC Dave's report, his work on the case had ended long ago. Moore testified that he never told anyone on that day that Terrance had attempted to run over Smulski. This was a sharp contradiction of what Smulski said under oath because she had basically blamed Moore for that particular radio communication. Moore admitted to having seen the apartment video months later, not before he prepared his report. He did endeavor to secure the video before completing his report but was not successful.

In his report, he noted Smulski "jumped" out of the way. This was a significant point to address especially since Smulski in essence alleged the same thing. I decided not to play the video for these three witnesses, but rather, save it for trial. But there was this exchange with Moore:

Q. You have that [his report] right in front of you?

A. Yes, sir.

Q. Did I read correctly you claim Sergeant Smulski was able to jump out of the way?

A. Yes you did, sir.

Q. So your memory is she jumped out of the way, correct?

A. That's correct, sir.

I now took a chance. I did not know what his answer would be, but this was a discovery deposition, not at trial in front of a jury. The jury only hears deposition testimony when a witness deviates from what they said at an earlier date. Utilizing the deposition testimony in the event of a different answer at a later date is a process known as impeachment. If I did not get the answer I wanted, so what.

Q. When you watch the video, did you see her jump out of the way?

A. No. She did not.

Q. So is that part of your report inaccurate?

A. The wording is inaccurate.

Brian Carter made an objection, but the damage was done. If this was all we got out of the Moore deposition, it was a huge success. Moore attempted to explain what he meant initially in his report, but he certainly admitted that the notion Smulski "jumped out of the way" was not accurate.

It was yet another example of the power of video. Moore honestly stated that a salient detail in his report was not accurate, but that was only upon seeing the video. I would note as an aside that if he did not make this admission, I was ready to play the video for him – and would have. The bottom line was that without the video, Moore would not have deviated from his report. People therefore would have been more inclined to believe Terrance tried to kill a cop.

Without video, the dead suspect had no voice – literally and figuratively. With video, the truth was coming out. Without video, the false narrative George Floyd died of a "medical" was likely to be believed. It was a miracle technology often used by citizens that spoke the truth – like in Franklin.

At one point during the Franklin investigation, Moore was shown the Gaines' video clip with a Commander Johnson. There was no attempt, to Moore's knowledge, to enhance the audio. Moore provided no help in his deposition as to the key content of what we claimed could be heard.

Moore's deposition supported the contention that Terrance had not attempted to run over Smulski, but that was not what the field cops were hearing that afternoon before Terrance was killed. This was further strong circumstantial evidence for murder, and this perception that Terrance had tried to run over and therefore kill a police officer was something we would certainly cover with the SWAT basement cops. But before those depositions, we would once again turn to DOC Dave for help.

DOC Dave had been tremendously helpful for the DNA problem. We were confident he would also have helpful information for the initial attempted apprehension, and we were right. Dave had arrived just before Smulski and Moore. He saw the PT Cruiser was occupied. He waited for the marked squads in part because his vehicle was an unmarked SUV.

He came up to the PT Cruiser strangely with his gun drawn. This alone could have scared Terrance into his later conduct. Dave saw there were passengers in the vehicle. His voice directives were ignored. Although he knew Terrance was only suspected of a crime at an earlier date and, as far as Dave knew, had not committed any serious crime or any crime at all that afternoon, Dave was nonetheless prepared to shoot him.

He testified that he believed Terrance was trying to run Smulski over as he tried to exit, but that allegation was not documented in his report. This was an obvious important fact to let others in the field know about if it was true, but he then gave these strange answers:

Q. Was it your belief he was trying to kill her?

A. Yes.

Q. . . . Did you tell other officers in the field that that's what you saw before the time that the guy was killed in the house?

A. I don't recall.

Q. I assume that was important to you, the fact that this guy had tried to intentionally kill a police officer. Wasn't that important?

A. Yes. But I wasn't the major person in charge of that stop or the major person that was relaying information to Minneapolis police. That would have been done by Sergeants Smulski and Moore.

So here is where we were at with DOC Dave: He thought Terrance was trying to kill Smulski, but he does not note that in his report nor does he radio that to other law enforcement in the field. We had the video for the jury. The point with all of this evidence combined together was that it was now clear Terrance did not try to kill anyone at the point of initial apprehension regardless of the apparent confusion of these witnesses. The video took away the confusion and made crystal clear that this was a young man, all told, who was merely trying to exit the parking lot to avoid apprehension. And maybe avoid getting killed since he knew he had done nothing wrong, but a cop was pointing a gun at him. So much for the notion of de-escalation. It seemed all three did not want to be stuck with the guilt that they told others in the field something that did not happen.

But Dave then said something else: He agreed with the notion that Terrance had "attempted to kill an officer" was in fact broadcast over the police radio airwaves. Dave then alleged that he was not the person who conveyed this message. He had no idea however who the source was.

We now had concrete evidence as to why there was a feeding frenzy in the Lyn-Lake neighborhood before Terrance was killed. Therefore, the recollections of Cala, Bam, Jim Bickal, and Anthony Oberlander were accurate. Regardless of how they came to their conclusions, MPD during the pursuit thought Terrance had tried to kill one of their own. These depositions with the video confirmed Terrance did not attempt to run over anyone. It seemed clear the MPD SWAT team probably thought otherwise even before they arrived at the scene and began the search. They had to be angry, but would they admit that? The lead homicide investigators Kjos and Porras conveniently failed to ask about that topic when they conducted their investigation, that is, were you mad when looking for this guy?

It seemed clear this detail we had obtained was all due to the pure luck that a surveillance camera had recorded the event. The SWAT team must have thought Terrance was an attempted cop killer. It was now time to find out their perspective about this topic and many others, and it would all be under oath.

Chapter Ten
The Basement

The argument could be made that at this point we had enough evidence not only to easily defeat the inevitable defense immunity motion for dismissal, but also to win at trial. Terrance had been murdered, and we were now confident that we knew why. We could at least give the jury a rational, sensible explanation.

We were confident going into the SWAT team depositions that they would not willingly admit anything, but we were equally confident that we could obtain testimony that would chip away at the defense and support our theories. To secure this type of evidence in the form of sworn testimony would be extremely important, certainly to help convince a jury that our version of events was perfectly valid. The key bullet points were that Durand had accidentally discharged the MP5, and Peterson and Meath had murdered Terrance out of pure retribution due in part to that negligent discharge, and also the incorrect belief that Terrance tried to kill a police officer with a car. The theory was competent, simple, and basic – which is how we liked it.

The depositions of the five would all take place at the end of August of 2015. I decided to depose Ricardo Muro first. Megan O'Connor, an associate attorney with Jay and Mike's firm, would attend the depositions with me. The depositions would take place over three long days.

Officer Muro sustained a significant injury to his right thigh/hip area from a single round of the powerful MP5. He was hurt so badly it was certainly understandable that his recall would not be as good as the others, but it was equally clear The Blue Code had not abandoned him.

He was a short man, Hispanic, and 38 years old. He had been with MPD since 2001 and began with SWAT in 2005. He was close to Lucas Peterson and had done things socially with him outside of work for years.

Questions were asked about his work history and his personnel file. Due to an order issued during the Franklin case, matters of this type with any officer cannot be disclosed in this book unless already a matter of public record through, for example, media reports. Other topics such as the date of birth of an officer, or the home address of the officer, cannot be disclosed herein.

Regarding the events of May 10, 2013, Muro recalled very little detail of the event. I did actually play the Gaines' video clip for him in the deposition, and he would admit only to hearing "officer shot." He stated that his injuries affected his ability to recall detail, but he did have some recall that was helpful to our case.

He agreed that he was not in the laundry room at the time Terrance was killed. I asked him specifically how much time elapsed from the time he was shot to the time Terrance was killed? He had no clue. He additionally could not even give an estimate as to how many rounds were fired when Terrance was killed. He did confirm for me that this time-gap question had never been asked by the homicide investigators.

He then said this after noting that the SWAT team was deployed from the downtown Minneapolis Haaf parking ramp:

Q. So what was it that prompted you guys to leave the Haaf ramp? What was it that you heard?

A. I remember hearing that the suspect had almost – had hit one of the squads and that he had almost hit Sergeant Smulski, ran over them.

Q. Ran over her?

A. Correct.

Q. How did you find out? Was that from dispatch?

A. I remember hearing it over the radio.

Q. Whose radio was that?

A. I don't remember. I believe it was 1280. The truck itself. The van itself.

So if Muro had heard it en route, the whole SWAT team should have heard it. This was an important, huge fact that fit right in with our theory as to what occurred that day. Would the other SWAT basement cops admit to hearing it?

After he got into the basement, it was completely dark. Since nobody on the team could find the wall switch, he turned his flashlight on. I asked who shot him:

Q. Is it your contention that you were shot by Mr. Franklin?

A. Yes.

Q. Are you sure of that?

A. I would say so, yes.

The reasonable interpretation of this answer was that he really did not know. It was not until later that he admitted that at the time of the event, he had no idea who had shot the MP5 for the single round that struck him.

His testimony was essentially consistent with his supplement as revealed in Chapter 4. He had no idea how or who killed Terrance. He was not sure if Stender and Nash were in the basement when Terrance was killed. He did allege he heard Durand say, "He has got a gun!" Muro said that Terrance never spoke. This was back to the Automaton Theory, which meant The Blue Code was in full regalia with Muro. We already knew that Terrance had uttered two sentences after the time that an officer was shot: "My name is Mookie"; and, "Man, let me go!"

Muro noted the interesting fact that he never at any time drew sight on the MP5 after he had entered the basement.

I next explored with him the issue of the laundry room door, which we knew from other evidence, may have in fact been closed when Terrance was killed. His testimony on this topic was all over the map. He claimed at one point it was closed, but he also alleged that it was closed during the "middle of the struggle." His contention was that it was accidentally closed and then open when he left the laundry room.

He then made the strange, not credible allegation, that at one point, all six men, including Franklin, were in the laundry room. The notion that could be true was almost impossible considering how small that room was. The dimension work up by MPD had that little room measured at 11' by 10" on the east side and 9' x 11" on the north side. The laundry room was located at the northwest quadrant of the basement. When one considered the two appliances and the sink that abutted the east side of the room, there was very little space with those items and the wall to the west. The room's door was located in the southwest quadrant of the room. Pictures taken of the room with Terrance's dead body in place revealed how small it was. Plus, I had been in it for Ed's testing. It was tiny.

Unbelievably, Muro testified that when all six were in the room, the door was closed, but then ended that testimony with the ambiguous words, "I would say."

Muro saw no one strike Terrance and had no idea how some of Terrance's dreads ended up apparently yanked out. He claimed the laundry room door was open when Terrance was killed, but then there was this exchange regarding how he, Muro, was shot:

> Q. You weren't in a position to tell anyone at the hospital about what specifically happened because you really didn't know. There was a fracas going on and all of a sudden, you are shot, right? Is that fair?
>
> A. Yes.

We now knew based on sworn testimony that one of the two officers who was shot on May 10, 2013 had no idea how it happened, and Chief Harteau had never disclosed this to the public. It was clear Muro could provide little help to the defense at the time of trial. It was equally clear that his knowledge provided more help to the plaintiff, our side, than the defendants.

The next witness would be Sergeant Andy Stender, the handler of K-9 Nash and the leader of the basement SWAT team. As a legal team, we were always intrigued by Stender and felt, reading through the lines, that he was probably mad at Peterson and Meath for what happened. No doubt there was a plan to beat up Terrance and allow Nash some bites. To a certain extent, that could be understood, if not condoned. Steve Rogers, who attended the basement SWAT team depositions, was completely on the same page with me regarding my thoughts about this witness and the other basement cops. Megan agreed also.

But was Stender down there with Terrance when they killed Terrance? All three of us felt he was not, and he was either going up the stairs or had already gone out the north side door at the time Terrance was executed. It was clear Stender was locked into The Blue Code from his Q&A, but we felt we could make some headway with him under oath.

Stender had the look of the Marlboro man, a shorter version, put together (strong), with a full mustache. (After this date, I would often see him working security at Minnesota Timberwolves' games.) On the way to and before he entered the basement, he alleged that he had never heard that the suspect had attempted to kill a police officer or had hit a squad with a car. I next covered if he had any knowledge as to how or why the MP5 discharged:

> Q. You are aware of the fact that there is a claim in this case that the MP5 discharged two times. You are aware of that, right?
>
> A. Yes, sir.
>
> Q. Do you have any idea where you were when that happened?
>
> A. I believe I was in the area of the laundry room door.

Q.   And you don't know how it was that firearm
     discharged, correct?

A.   That's correct.

If that was all we got out of Stender, it would have been a
successful day. But we were able to get more.

I asked him the big question about the time gap from the MP5
discharge to Terrance being killed. We jockeyed back and forth. He
first said, "Short amount of time." He then later committed to my
question of less than ten seconds. I asked him about Sporny's estimate
of a gap of between 20-30 seconds. He said, "I don't know what the
time frame was. It was a short amount of time, but I can't answer
anything specifically like that."

Stender admitted first seeing Terrance behind the water heater
– an important admission - because Terrance never should have ended
up in the laundry room with that fact alone. Nash had bitten on to
Terrance's sweatshirt. Stender used his flashlight to strike Terrance.
He also had him in a headlock.

I next addressed the issue of the laundry room door. I asked
Stender if the door was closed up until the time Terrance was killed.
He said, "It was open until I pulled out Officer Muro. And then I
remembered that the door was closed at that time. It was open prior to
that." Stender then alleged that Peterson, Durand, and Meath were in
the laundry room with the door closed when Terrance was killed. We
expected him to say they were in the laundry room, but the notion that
the door was closed was a shocking and important revelation to
support our theory of execution. We felt we could easily prove with
other evidence that there was no way that Durand could have been in
that room at the time of the execution. Stender then had to admit that
with the door closed, he would have had no idea how or who killed
Terrance.

I played the Gaines' video clip for him, and like Muro, he gave
nothing except that he could hear "officer shot." He gave the not
surprising answer that as part of the official investigation, he was
never asked about Jimmy Gaines or the video at all.

Stender did not give his Q&A until three days after May 10,
and Fred Bruno, the Federation's attorney, was present. Stender told

96

me about the meeting with Bruno earlier that day, and the other attendees were Durand, Peterson, and two other SWAT members named Valencia and Staufenberg. Brian Carter asserted attorney-client privilege for what was discussed, but I just wanted to prove the meeting did in fact happen, and it was before Stender or any of the others had given their Q&A. Stender did readily admit this, but he could not recall how long the meeting was. This type of meeting was known as a "sandpaper job." Sandpaper the rough edges, i.e., come up with a story. We felt this meeting was the birth of the Automaton Theory.

The obvious point we would make for the jury was that they all got together to get their story straight, and briefing Muro and Meath later would be easy. Like Muro, the Stender deposition had been fruitful. We were hopeful for the same with the remaining three: Meath, Durand, and Peterson.

I deposed Michael Meath the same day as Stender. Meath, a handsome man, was of average build, but strong like Stender. He appeared to be a weightlifter. He began with MPD in 2005, almost exactly 10 years before this deposition, and entered SWAT in 2010.

Megan was again present to assist, and I recall her telling me when we were done that Meath "creeped her out." Overall, there was something about his demeanor that was strange, and his answers at times almost seemed robotic. He claimed ignorance for various topics he should have had answers to. His answers were often one word or very short along the lines of "I don't remember" or "not that I recall." I did not find him credible. Of course, that would be for the jury to decide.

Meath was shot in the right leg at the time of the incident. Durand, Peterson, and Stender came to see him in the hospital along with hundreds of cops who came to see him at this home after he was discharged. It appeared that getting shot and killing Terrance had lifted him to hero status. The SWAT basement cops also went to visit him at his home, except for Muro, due to his extended hospital stay.

Meath's Q&A was not until 11 days after the incident. He had met with an attorney prior to giving a statement, and his attorney was present for that process. The Stender, Durand, and Peterson statements were over a week before, but he claimed that he had not

97

been briefed on those before he gave his statement. At trial, we would ask the jury if that made sense or was believable.

He was never presented with an enhanced version of the Gaines' video. He claimed the N-word was not used by him or any SWAT member in the Franklin incident. He noted that Terrance said nothing at all during the struggle from beginning to end, a huge contradiction with the Gaines' video clip. It was clear to us that Meath was in the strong grip of The Blue Code.

Before Meath was aware that he was shot, he recalled hearing one boom and really had no idea what led up to the MP5 discharging or how or why it discharged. This was the same for Muro and Stender.

> Q. And at some point did you hear the gun [the MP5] discharge?
>
> A. I did.
>
> Q. You don't know the specific circumstances as to how the gun discharged?
>
> A. Correct.

Even though he had killed Terrance with Peterson, he provided no time estimate as to the time gap from him being shot to the time he killed the suspect. After hearing "one boom," he gave these answers:

> Q. And did you immediately feel pain at that point?
>
> A. I did.
>
> Q. What I want to ask you, sir, is from the time you heard that discharge, how much time elapsed to the time Franklin was killed?
>
> A. I wouldn't be able to give you an exact number.
>
> Q. Was it quick?

A. I mean, the whole situation was dynamic and very fast.

Q. Was it within seconds?

A. Again, I told you I couldn't give you an exact number.

It was clear that as part of the official investigation, Meath had never been asked about the time gap. His answers on this topic were tantamount to an admission that the Gaines' clip was a problem for the defendants.

Meath was close to Peterson even long before their jobs with MPD. They had even played high school hockey together.

Meath claimed he heard nothing en route to the scene about the suspect having attempted to run over an MPD cop. This was a sharp contradiction from what Muro had said in his deposition. He treated the Franklin incident as just another event. He claimed that the team was not amped up on the way to the scene. How could that be true if some of the team members were aware that the suspect had tried to kill a fellow officer? We as a team of course did not believe Meath on this issue. It was our belief that the entire SWAT team, even those who had not entered the basement, had the mindset that Terrance was an attempted cop killer.

Around the time Terrance was killed, Meath did not recall Peterson giving any voice commands. He claimed nobody struck Terrance, but supporting the Automaton Theory, he claimed Terrance did not react to being bitten by Nash and did not seem to be in pain.

Meath claimed he was in an altercation with Terrance, Terrance broke away, and then Terrance was in a struggle with Durand and Peterson. Meath alleged he lost sight of them, but then somehow ended up in the laundry room with the three. He noted that he did not hear Peterson fire his gun, and he did not see muzzle flash from Peterson's gun either. It was not until later that evening that he found out that Peterson had fired too. This answer was bizarre. Was Meath even there?

He did recall firing his gun but could not say when or how far away the suspect was when he shot him. He admitted that Terrance was on the ground seated when shot, an important fact for our

99

execution theory. He said that Terrance's right side was facing him as he shot Terrance.

I then decided to approach the time gap in a different fashion: From the time he felt pain up until the time he killed Terrance. His response was: "Again, I am not good with numbers." Meath claimed ignorance as to how some of Terrance's dreads ended up yanked out.

The dust had now settled from Meath's story. We were now 3 for 3. No basement cop to this point – Muro, Stender, and Meath – had any idea how the MP5 discharged. This was good news for our case going into the Durand and Peterson depositions.

Tim Skarda, the senior defense attorney, would handle Durand's deposition at their office. Skarda handling this one was a message to us that they understood it was extremely important. Durand was small in stature, wore glasses, and was professorial in appearance. He was 46 years old, 5'4", and weighed 145 pounds. He had been employed with MPD for 15 years.

His quotes after the killing to the sergeant and to DOC Dave, when juxtaposed with Muro, Stender, and Meath that they had no clue why or how his MP5 discharged, was strong evidence to support accidental or negligent discharge. Considering Peterson's history of excessive force and dishonesty, along with his Q&A painting himself to be a hero, we felt a reasonable juror would not believe anything he said of substance.

Could Durand dig himself out of this hole? We were about to find out. After I began, I learned up front, to nobody's surprise, that as part of the official investigation, Durand had never been asked any questions at all about the Gaines' video clip. Therefore, he was not asked what he could or could not hear, and as of this day in August of 2015, he literally had never watched the video at all.

Again, it was not a surprise that he was never asked by the homicide investigators about the timing of events such as how much time elapsed from the time his gun, the MP5, discharged to the time Meath and Peterson killed Terrance.

When he gave his Q&A, attorney Fred Bruno was present. Durand confirmed that the meeting with Bruno on May 13 with the other SWAT team members, except Muro and Meath, was before he gave his statement. He also believed that was a time frame before any basement SWAT team member had given a statement.

Early in the deposition, I asked him about the Green Bay debacle with Thole and Powell. I wanted to gauge his honesty. Both were members of the same precinct as Durand, the 4th. He knew both but claimed no special close relationship with either.

He noted that there was a department policy that derogatory or racist terms like the N-word could not be used in the field. He admitted that he knew about the Green Bay incident, but then alleged, amazingly, that Thole and Powell had never said anything negative or racist about black people in his presence. I then asked him about the other SWAT members who had entered the basement: "What about Peterson? Did you ever hear Peterson in the field use a derogatory term directed towards black people?"

"No."

"What about Meath?"

"No."

"What about Muro?"

"No."

"What about Stender?"

"No."

The answers were not surprising, but I had to ask. However, I did note a change in his demeanor from this point forward. The questions I was asking made clear I knew the case file, and I would not leave any stone unturned. The deposition would be long. After transcribed, it ended up to be 160 pages in length. Durand was nervous. Even though he was deep into the cover-up, I felt sympathy for him. He was not a murderer. He was placed into a no-win situation. We felt that if he did not support this monumentally absurd story, he could be disciplined, and two people he had been close to for years, both personally and professionally, could be prosecuted for murder. He would also be ostracized forever by the universe of police officers and probably lose his job for lying in an official police investigation. The Blue Code had its grip on him and would not let go. There was also the fact he accidentally injured two of his own guys. Better to blame the black suspect.

Durand said he was "very surprised" when he heard of the conduct of Thole and Powell in Green Bay. Was this the only time these men went on a racist rant in their entire life? Would any reasonable juror believe Durand if this came up at trial?

Durand admitted a social relationship with Peterson. Of the other four, he was closest to Meath. Durand described MPD SWAT as "a close group of guys." As of August of 2015, not one member of the unit was a woman.

Durand admitted that he knew Dave Schiebel well and knew of him as "DOC Dave." He was on a first name basis with Dave, and he noted that Dave had worked with MPD often. Durand was at the Haaf Ramp downtown when he heard his team was needed. Regarding the MP5 that he had with him that day, he described it as having a collapsible stock, and when he used it in the field, it would not be fully extended. He made the harness he used for it from scratch. He also had on his person that day a holstered Sig Sauer handgun. He admitted that he easily could kill someone with that handgun in seconds.

The words he heard that prompted the SWAT team to deploy were "a vehicle pursuit." He recalled hearing Sergeant Moore's voice through the radio of the SWAT vehicle. Durand specifically also heard that the suspect had intentionally tried to injure a fellow officer.

Q. Did Sergeant Moore reference a suspect?

A. He said the suspect driver had nearly struck another 5th Precinct supervisor.

. . .

Q. Was it your understanding that he had attempted to intentionally injure that person or did you have any thought process that way?

A. That's the way it sounded on the radio, yes.

En route, he was with Meath, Muro, Valencia, Staufenberg, and Laux. Strangely, Peterson was not present, but it would seem obvious to us as a team that the others who heard it would have told Peterson. Durand denied Moore's communication got his adrenalin more pumped up. Whether it made him angry, he responded with: "Didn't make me happy." He did concede however that it made the call "more

102

important." He took Moore at his word. As of this date, Durand said that he still had not seen the apartment video.

Durand claimed that the Moore radio comm did not change the demeanor of the SWAT members in the van. He admitted to a sense of urgency with the notion that the suspect tried to run over an officer. He learned the suspect was African American and received a description of the suspect's clothing. There was no data from any source that the suspect was armed.

After arriving at the scene, the team split up to search "yard to yard." They soon learned of the broken rear door at 2717 Bryant and then entered the home at that location. He provided the interesting fact that at no point before they eventually entered the basement did anyone on the team ask the homeowner how to turn the lights on for the basement.

I asked Durand if any of the SWAT team members had gloves on, and he said that he did not know. I then asked this important question, "Did anyone else who came into the basement after Franklin had been killed have gloves on?"

"I don't know."

This was the type of question and answer that would seem innocuous in a case unless one knew the full story. There was, of course, one specific reason I asked this question: DOC Dave. Durand now would not be able to rescue DOC Dave to support the notion DOC Dave had gloves on after the suspect was killed, a contention we knew was specious in light of the fact that Dave's DNA was on the MP5 in multiple places. Durand would be in a position to know since he handed the MP5 directly to Dave. Perhaps a little thing, but it was these little things combined together that were supporting our overall theory that Franklin was murdered, not killed by police officers just doing a competent job in the line of duty.

Durand signaled to the others that he heard movement in the basement. It would not be long before they had direct contact with the suspect. Durand recalled that he went down the steps side by side with Stender. The small laundry room was to the left at the bottom of the steps. It had a door, and the door was open. Durand confirmed the laundry room was small and then noted at some point during the struggle the door ended up closed, but he was unsure of its open or closed status when Terrance was killed.

The K-9 found Terrance behind the water heater under the steps. Durand claimed Terrance stood up after the dog bit onto him. Durand then expectedly supported the Automaton Theory, consistent with his Q&A: Durand believed the dog bit the suspect, but the suspect did not show any sign of pain. Durand claimed Nash was trying to pull the suspect out while at the same time, Stender was striking the suspect in the face.

Durand alleged that the suspect was not complying but did confirm that there was no indication the suspect had a weapon. He never saw Terrance physically strike or hit anyone.

Durand supported his Q&A and opined that he ended up in the laundry room with Peterson, Meath, and Terrance. He then claimed that Meath said: "What are you grabbing for? My gun?" I then asked Durand about the laundry room. I questioned him about how it was that Terrance was first located behind the water heater near the bottom of the steps and then ended up in the laundry room.

> Q. What I am trying to figure out, sir – and help me with this. With five guys down there and a police dog, how was it that this guy [Terrance] was able to move from that area to the laundry room?
>
> A. I don't know.

This was probably the best answer he could have given. Any other answer would not have made any sense so he went down the path of least resistance. He did however claim that Terrance tackled him "like a football tackle." Durand claimed that during the tackle was the time when Terrance was somehow able to reach out and squeeze the trigger of the MP5. Even though the MP5 was in a harness that he had made, Durand claimed Terrance ended up with a hand on the gun's grip.

Two rounds went off. Durand could not say if the suspect aimed the gun, which was in semi-automatic mode.

I asked Durand about accidental discharge. He had never been trained on it and strangely claimed that an MP5 could not be accidentally shot. He seemed to not know or understand the concept at all. This answer bordered on laughable. Any gun could be accidentally shot, a fact folks were reminded of when an Australian woman was killed by one round at the hands of an MPD cop in July of 2017, not far from the neighborhood where Terrance was killed.

After the MP5 discharged (Durand claimed caused by the suspect), he said that Officer Peterson fired his sidearm and killed the suspect. It was unclear to Durand in the moment, in real time, if anyone else fired their gun.

The mystery of the yanked-out dreads continued. Durand did not see Peterson grab Terrance's hair. Why was this important? We felt it was the means by which Peterson and Meath dragged Terrance into the laundry room to be executed. It was convenient how nobody knew about the dreads.

I asked again about the time frame since Durand's description made it sound quick.

> Q. . . . After Franklin tackled you into the laundry room, it sounds to me like this was a very quick scenario. That then Peterson stepped in and killed Franklin. Correct?
>
> A. Peterson came in and fired his weapon.
>
> Q. Right away though, right?
>
> A. I don't know the time frame.
>
> Q. You can't give me any help on the time frame, sir?
>
> A. No.

It was amazing what a taboo subject the time gap had become for almost every key witness in the case. It was obvious to our legal team that each basement SWAT cop had been closely counseled about the time gap issue. Durand did allege he yelled out to the others "he's got a gun" after he claimed Terrance accessed his, that is, the MP5.

Durand said Terrance was physically engaged with him and Peterson when Peterson killed Terrance. He claimed he was on the ground with Terrance when Peterson straddled over them and shot. At that time, Durand claimed Terrance was lying across his legs.

As a team, we felt that the notion that Durand knew nothing about Meath firing was further evidence that he was not in the laundry room when Terrance was killed. He did however finally admit that the process of Terrance being killed was like one fluid event and said in response to this question: "So at the time he was killed, your perception was that it was just you and Peterson and Franklin, correct?

"Yes."

I then went through the litany of the key words from the Gaines' video clip by actually playing it for him. Like the others, he admitted to hearing only, "officer shot," and nothing else.

Durand confirmed there was blood on his clothing from the incident with the fight in close quarters. We had already reached the obvious conclusion that there was no way the MP5 could be blood free if it was in the middle of this melee. Durand confirmed the MP5 never left his body due to the harness.

I then asked him about the Sergeant Strauss quote.

> Q. You did speak with Sergeant Strauss about what happened, right?
>
> A. Yes.
>
> Q. Did you tell him, and I quote, "It was my gun, Sarge", close quote. Did you say that to him?
>
> A. I don't recall.

I then showed him a copy of the Strauss report, Supplement #99, and I asked him to read it. Upon reading it, he admitted that he had in fact said that. This was of course a huge admission. I decided to not ask him why he said it. In some situations, such as this one, discretion is the better part of valor. The idea or point was to get him to admit he said it, and I had achieved that goal. It made no sense to belabor the point.

Before the deposition, my team and I made a strategy decision as a team to not ask Durand about his quote to DOC Dave when he said, according to Dave: "This is the gun that caused the injuries." What Dave said was hearsay, but it was a clear exception to the hearsay rule such that it would be admitted into evidence. The exceptions were "statement of a party opponent" or perhaps in the category of an "admission of a party opponent". The admission we alleged was that with that quote, it was Durand in essence admitting that he negligently discharged the gun. Our thought was why give Durand a chance to explain away the obvious?

In a case like this, we would have the right to call MPD personnel in our case and ask them questions in cross-examination mode, the leading-question format. An example of that would be, "Isn't it true, Officer Durand, that after Terrance Franklin was killed, you handed your gun to Dave Schiebel and said, 'This is the gun that caused the injuries.'" Then in follow-up: "And the reason you said that, sir, is the truth of the matter is that you accidentally shot that gun, didn't you?" As the reader may have noticed up to this point, my questions were more open-ended in the discovery depositions. In this process, it is typically a format of questioning different than at trial in part because the lawyer is exploring for information. Durand would face aggressive questions at the time of trial but not now. The bottom line is that what DOC Dave said when he was handed the gun would be believed. DOC Dave was arguably our most important witness. He was the gift that kept giving.

Stender, Muro, and Meath had no idea how the MP5 discharged. Now Durand made two inculpatory comments just after the incident that made no sense unless he accidentally fired the gun in the middle of a fracas. So what would Peterson say about all of this? We would soon find out.

The deposition of Lucas Peterson was the last one of substance before the inevitable immunity motion of our opponents. We decided to videotape this one.

Peterson had the appearance of a tough dude. He was wearing a suit and had a clean-cut appearance. He was of average size, 35 years old, was born and raised in Minneapolis, and began his employment with MPD in 2000. He testified to his Caucasian ethnicity the same as Stender, Meath, and Durand. He began with MPD SWAT in 2003.

I found Peterson to be the most intelligent witness of all of the MPD field cops. He seemed intent on convincing me that he had done nothing wrong on May 10, 2013. He was not confrontational and was in fact respectful. My perception of the man was that he was grateful that he had gotten away with this, and if there was civil liability, so be it. His employer would cover that expense like the Burns', Simmons', and Johnson matters previously reported in the *Strib* stories. Those matters were addressed in the deposition but cannot be addressed in this book due to the confidentiality order.

Peterson gave the scarcely credible answer that he was not a racist. So I then hit him with the Green Bay incident, and his answer was such that Thole and Powell were saints and never showed racist tendencies in performance of their MPD SWAT duties. Peterson was "shocked" when he heard about the Green Bay details. We silently laughed at that answer.

He confirmed the meeting with Fred Bruno and the other SWAT team members on May 13, and the convenient fact that the meeting took place before he gave his statement to the homicide investigators.

The first time he had ever watched or listened to the Gaines' video clip was the week before preparing for his deposition. It was amazing how these officers in essence claimed complete ignorance about this important piece of evidence. Peterson never endeavored to watch it on YouTube, although he was aware of its existence.

His firearm on May 10, a Sig Sauer, had been holstered. He was wearing his standard blue issued uniform, perfect attire for The Blue Code of Silence.

Peterson heard by radio that the suspect was wanted for burglary and "crashing" into a police car. He did not recall anything about the suspect attempting to run over a police officer. He gave answers such that even if that were true, it would not be relevant to him. Nonetheless, he did not have the mindset that he was dealing with a suspect who had tried to injure a police officer. The atmosphere in the van on the way to the scene amazingly was "light and jovial." Although this man was smart, this type of answer was really hurting his credibility and bordered on laughable.

The team arrived at 28th and Aldrich or Bryant, not far from the Bickal home at 2717 Bryant. As they were checking from house to house, they received word the suspect could be in 2717 Bryant. The team then went to the back of the Bickal home, and then eventually entered in the rear.

108

I decided to jump ahead and ask Peterson about the time gap. This answer alone was really all we needed since we expected him to stay consistent with his Q&A. The last thing we wanted was some type of answer along the lines of a rational explanation for why or if there was a significant delay between the MP5 discharge and the killing of the suspect. Peterson did not disappoint. After establishing that Durand's MP5 discharged, and that he, Peterson, subsequently killed the suspect, I asked Peterson about the time gap.

> Q. How much time elapsed, sir, from the time that the MP5 discharged to the time Franklin was killed?
>
> A. Short amount of time.
>
> Q. Matter of seconds?
>
> A. Yes.

This is what we wanted. It was really the first time any basement SWAT cop committed to a specific time frame. That answer of course could not be reconciled with the Gaines' video clip at all. Peterson had fallen into the trap.

Peterson assumed Terrance was in the basement since Durand had heard movement down there. As they made their way down, Peterson confirmed the north side door was closed. He initially went down with Stender and Durand. He corroborated Nash finding Terrance and then the free-for-all was on. Peterson confirmed the other officers' testimony that Nash found Terrance by the water heater. Nash bit Terrance, and Stender punched him. Peterson alleged that the suspect "just kind of stood there vacant to that blow." Stender then struck Terrance with the flashlight. Peterson confirmed staying perfectly consistent with his statement.

Peterson alleged noncompliance, but then described Terrance as "passively resistant." He claimed Terrance was never successfully apprehended, another sharp contradiction from the Gaines' video. Peterson then described a "charging bull" scenario and that the suspect was "throwing punches." We finally now had an admission regarding the dreads: Peterson grabbed them and pulled some out.

109

Durand said Terrance did not strike or punch anyone, another huge contradiction from Peterson.

Confirming the Automaton Theory, Peterson claimed that Durand was tackled into the laundry room. Peterson found both on the ground. Strangely, Peterson did not hear the MP5 discharge. He was then asked this:

> Q. So you don't know the circumstances on how the gun went off?
>
> A. I don't.

Nobody could corroborate Durand's story as to how the MP5 was fired. Under these facts, for us and our client, that was tantamount to a miracle. But strangely, Peterson then alleged that Terrance had control of the MP5, and Peterson could see that with his flashlight. The MP5 was pointed at him. Peterson claimed Terrance did not fire. Peterson then made the decision to kill the suspect. He claimed he fired five times when Terrance was "an arm's reach away." Peterson aimed at the head. He thought he was the only person shooting.

I established the important point that there was a lot of blood in the laundry room area where Terrance was killed, and there was blood all over Peterson too. I confirmed with Peterson that portion of his statement where it was noted that he was "covered in blood." He did in fact clean off some of the blood before pictures were later taken by FS personnel.

Peterson then gave the interesting answer that he was resting on the MP5 when Terrance was killed. The gun of course was found later by FS Hummel and FS Jacobson - with no blood on it.

Peterson denied using the N-word in his interaction with the suspect. He also could not say if Stender was in the basement when he killed Franklin.

Next, the issue of the laundry room door was addressed. I was able to secure a wonderful admission, which we did not think we would get. Steve Rogers attended the deposition with Megan and me, and we were downright giddy after the deposition due to these answers:

110

Q. Was there ever a point during this process that the laundry room door was closed?

A. Yes.

Q. At what point in time, sir?

A. I found it closed after I was trying to get Officer Meath out of the basement.

. . .

Q. . . . After you killed Franklin, you then at some point exited the laundry room? Correct?

A. Yes.

Q. Wasn't it open then?

A. No.

Q. Do you have any idea when it was closed, sir?

A. I don't know when it was closed.

Peterson was in a quandary because there was other evidence to indicate it was in fact closed. With his testimony alone, we could fill in certain blanks to support our scenario: Terrance had surrendered according to the Gaines' video. Peterson had grabbed him by the hair, dragged him in the laundry room, and when Terrance was killed by both Peterson and Peterson's long-time friend Meath, it was probable that the laundry room door was closed. Why? So that none of the others would see their dirty deed. The high school buddies had killed a black man they thought had tried to kill one of their own about 90 minutes before. In their minds, we presumed, Peterson and Meath thought that was justice.

I later took the deposition of Mark Kaspszak. He was Peterson's partner for the Simmons'/Johnson incident as reported by the *Strib*. This officer was honest, namely, that Nancy Johnson had never assaulted him.

There were other depositions that should be briefly mentioned. Since Thole and Powell were fired, we were hopeful maybe we could get some honesty out of them regarding the racist ways of MPD SWAT. We were not successful. They basically had two themes: Lucas Peterson was the greatest human ever born, and they downplayed the events in Green Bay.

Thole testified that he never said "too nigger friendly" in Green Bay. He also said the reference to "doing the monkey" thing did not concern black people. In addition to claiming Powell never used the N-word in Green Bay, he claimed he never said the word on video. Powell however admitted to using the N-word "one time." He supported his friend Thole's contention that Thole did not say "Green Bay is too nigger friendly." Both depositions were characterized by one mistruth after another, an avalanche of perjury.

We decided to depose SWAT officer, Steven Laux. He was there on May 10 but did not go in the basement. I found him to be honest. He confirmed the Bruno meeting on May 13 but also noted a meeting with the SWAT team at City Hall on the evening of the incident minus Muro and Meath. It seemed clear the false narratives began that evening and formed the basis for the early MPD disclosures as to how the event went down. Laux also disclosed this interesting fact: He checked for signs of life on Terrance's body - without gloves. This was a wonderful admission for our theory.

SWAT officer John Staufenberg was deposed also. He freely admitted that on the way to the scene, he heard over the SWAT van radio that the suspect had rammed a vehicle and had tried to run over an officer. It was easy to see how killing Terrance could result in a hero label for Peterson and Meath. Staufenberg additionally confirmed the Bruno attorney meeting on May 13 since he was present.

Regarding the lead homicide investigators, we decided to depose Ann Kjos but not Louis Porras because Kjos handled all of the Q&A's. We felt this way even though Porras was lead. Kjos testified that it was her first investigation involving a citizen who had been killed by officers from her own agency. She claimed she maintained her objectivity but noted facts such as she had known Andy Stender

112

since she joined the force in 1988. She became a sergeant in 1996 and that was still her rank when I deposed her in September of 2015.

As part of the investigation, she knew nothing about the Burns', Simmons', and Johnson matters as they pertained to Lucas Peterson. She did not look into any prior civil claims, if any, of the five-member SWAT team that entered the basement.

Other than securing the Gaines' video clips from YouTube and placing them into evidence in the case file, she confirmed that neither she nor anyone with MPD did anything with the Gaines' video, not even attempting to hear what was on it on her own without expert enhancement. This answer was frankly shocking. Nobody above her rank gave her any directives regarding it. It was true. This was official confirmation that MPD had treated that evidence as if it did not exist for the official investigation. Kjos never even prepared a report about it. She additionally confirmed never interviewing Gaines.

She noted that MPD does not recognize GSR testing. That was it. The golden opportunity to determine if Terrance had actually shot a gun on the afternoon of May 10, 2013 was forever gone. Even former chief Tim Dolan, the MPD chief from 2006-2012, recognized GSR as valid under oath in his deposition.

Kjos provided the interesting fact that as each of the cops gave their Q&A, they were immediately given a copy of the transcription ostensibly to sign off on it. Therefore, it was obvious that Peterson, for example, could have seen the Q&A's of Stender and Durand in writing, which were one day before his on May 14, 2013. So much for the investigation having any integrity.

She never uncovered any evidence that the time gap between the MP5 discharging and Terrance being killed was anything other than quick. She expected it to be quick under these facts. It was clear that she had completely ignored the Gaines' video, which revealed a large gap. Regarding Officer Sporny who had the gap between 20-30 seconds, she did one of two things: Did not realize the significance of the gap or was aware of it and chose to completely ignore it because it went against the MPD narrative. To do something like this would be unconscionable, but the other option would indicate shocking incompetence. I felt the scenario that she was aware of the problem and chose to ignore it was more likely. This was a classic example of why in-house investigations were a really bad idea.

113

Regarding the initial attempted apprehension at the Lyndale apartment complex, Smulski never told her that Terrance had tried to kill her. Moore never told her that either.

She never uncovered any evidence that racist terms were used by SWAT with the Franklin incident. That answer could be understood since she never endeavored to have the Gaines' video clip enhanced even though I made the N-word allegation publicly within weeks of May 10, 2013. She had every incentive to prove me wrong. She did not even try. Maybe she did not want to know.

And this was the investigation that County Attorney Freeman called "professional."

We deposed former chief, Tim Dolan. I found him to be honest, and I liked him. He seemed to be a man who was handling retirement well. We were interested primarily on how he dealt with Lucas Peterson after the Simmons'/Johnson incident. For the reason of the confidentiality order, there are limitations as to what can be disclosed regarding Chief Dolan's testimony. What is contained here was submitted to the court as part of the summary judgment motion and the appeal, and therefore, a matter of public record.

Dolan confirmed for me that an MPD officer lying in an official report – which is exactly what Peterson did – was a fireable offense. At one point, he had an interview with WCCO, Channel 4, regarding the Franklin incident and Peterson. Dolan had a "sit down" with Peterson for on-the-job matters at some point prior to 2012. He recalled that there was some discipline assessed, but he could not recall what specifically.

I also deposed Chief Harteau. I felt bad for her because I thought it was possible the Franklin homicide investigators had duped her. I felt that she was honest in the deposition. Unbeknownst to anyone, she was less than two years away from being fired as fallout for the Justine Damond matter as detailed in a later chapter.

She provided the interesting testimony that she did request enhancement of the Gaines' video, but nobody in her agency had that ability. She never ordered that the video be secured directly from the citizen or that an outside expert be retained for enhancement.

I felt from her testimony that it was her belief that the entire matter should have been handled by an outside agency. Even as of this late date, she believed that Terrance had attempted to run over a police officer.

Discovery was over. We would now address the immunity motion of the defense, which we were confident we could defeat. Next would be trial, we thought, but our opponent had other plans.

Chapter Eleven

Jamar, Laquon, and the Motion

We received our final expert reports in October. Richard Ernest had determined a downward angle of gunfire declination at the time Terrance was killed. Since both Peterson and Meath admitted that Terrance was on the ground when they killed him, Ernest's work supported the idea of a cold-blooded execution.

Chuck Drago, our excessive force law enforcement expert, concluded the obvious – that the conduct of the officers in question was one of excessive force. He also concluded the sounds at second 53 of the Gaines' clip were in fact gunshots. Considering his many years' history as an assistant chief and police chief in Florida, and also as a cop who had often heard gunshots in the field and in gun ranges, we felt confident his belief in this regard would go into evidence.

Our computer expert Sean Harrington confirmed the sounds on Gaines' video including that "officer shot" matched, as he described it, the "metadata of the timestamp of the amateur video" and was accurate within one second of real time of the police radio data. He did support the contention that what we felt were gunshots at second 53 was "a separate and distinct sound from the jet aircraft engine."

Our sound guy, Ed Primeau, had some interesting conclusions. At second nine, we always felt we could hear Mookie. Ed's work concluded that starting at second eight, this could be heard: "My name is Mookie." That was great news for us. We were fully aware we could not get what he heard into evidence, but this would give us a good faith basis for asking witnesses questions using these words. We were aware our opponent would object, but that would be denied. This further supported surrender and apprehension.

At second 26, Ed noted: "Damn freakin' . . ." We felt the N-word was after that, but Ed could not reach that conclusion.

At second 27, he reported: " . . . let me go." This was close to what we had with the exception of "man" in the beginning. This of course was the voice of Terrance after he had been called the N-word, we believed. Many would testify at trial that this was his voice.

The next big wording was at second 43. We had: "Come out, little nigger! Don't go putting those hands up now!" We were confident this was Peterson expressing his frustration for the whole situation including the fact two of his guys had just been accidentally shot. Ed had: "Come out . . . put those hands up now." The words he did not give us he claimed to be unintelligible. We were not concerned. We were not disappointed. The jury would hear the enhanced version and, we felt, agree with our contentions as to what could be heard. Plus, what we claimed was sensible. Terrance said his name because he had been asked his name after being apprehended. Considering other situations where MPD used the N-word in social settings, it would not be surprising that they would use that word with Terrance because they thought he tried to run over a cop along with the additional circumstance that two cops were accidentally shot. They would not have been in that position had Terrance not given up sooner, a significant factor for their anger.

At second 27, Terrance asks to be let go because they are calling him the N-word. And at second 43, they let him go a few seconds previously to take care of at least one of the injured officers, and Terrance probably backed up into a corner or some such spot. He was then asked to come out, probably by Peterson, and he confirmed his capitulation by putting his hands up. That got Peterson more angry. It should be noted that there was a plethora of evidence I have only slightly touched on herein to indicate Meath did not realize he was shot until after Terrance had been killed.

Folks had inquired if a template of Peterson's voice could be obtained to compare it to the recording. Ed told us that type of testing was not possible.

Ed additionally concluded his testing regarding the gunshots was inconclusive. This was not troublesome. Harrington would note the change in sound quality, and Drago would say they were gunshots. We felt a lay jury would conclude they were gunshots, and the fact this sound location was eight seconds after the beginning of the last voice directive made sense. There was then nothing after that up to the end, second 62. That gave Peterson and Meath plenty of time to drag Terrance a very short distance into the laundry room, close the door, and then begin shooting him. The point was it all tied together, and we felt would make sense to Judge Frank for the defense motion and a jury at trial.

Not long after we completed discovery, two other high-profile killings by police of young black males occurred – one locally by MPD officers and one in Chicago, Illinois - which would become one of the highest profile excessive force cases in U.S. history.

On Sunday, November 15, 2015, a 24 year-old black male named Jamar Clark was shot in the early morning hours in Minneapolis. Two MPD officers were involved, and it was claimed that Clark was unarmed. The story went like this: After midnight on that Sunday, two MPD officers responded to a call for assistance from paramedics. The allegation was that a man was interfering with their ability to help an assault victim. Clark was the suspect in the assault of the woman who was receiving the treatment. During the encounter with the two officers, Clark was shot. There was speculation that Clark was cuffed at the time. MPD disputed this, but there were witnesses at the scene who alleged otherwise. There was also a witness, a black man, who claimed that Clark was not resisting before he was shot.

Protests began with the shutting down of interstates – protesters would walk right onto them – and the 4th Precinct in North Minneapolis had a sit-in protest that lasted for weeks. Chief Harteau and Mayor Hodges, realizing the severity of this from the perspective of people of color in Minneapolis, requested a federal investigation and a separate investigation by the Minnesota BCA. It was clear the concept of an in-house investigation by MPD for citizens killed at the hands of their officers was now a thing of the past.

A Black Lives Matter banner was actually hanging at one point on the entrance of the precinct, and MPD eventually got rid of that and then cordoned off an area around the precinct to create a distance between the protesters and the building. It was a cold time of the year so the protestors started to create bonfires and put up tents and other shelters to deal with the cold.

The Clark matter was a significant precursor to George Floyd with similar features except, and this was a big except, there was no video of substance, and the two MPD officers who were involved with the death of Clark did not have body cams. Early on, Harteau declined to say if squad cams or any other type of video had picked up the killing. This of course led to the possibility of a false narrative since without video, there was no technological clarity.

The situation outside of the precinct at times got ugly, and there were near riots. Images of officers pointing guns at the protesters who appeared to be of all races, but mostly African American, were often featured in the papers and on local television for weeks.

Stories came out about Clark's background, and the facts of the situation regarding his death were confusing. This was another event that put significant pressure on all police agencies in Minnesota, not just MPD, to move forward with mandatory body-cam use. From my perspective, body cams not only protected citizens, they also protected the police from false accusations. The last thing I wanted to do was to pursue an excessive force claim against a member of law enforcement that was not valid. With body cams, there probably would have been no gray area as to the facts leading up to and the actual shooting of Clark.

The narrative that eventually came out, and I was not surprised at all, was that Clark was reaching for a cop's gun, and that was why he was shot. Activist/reporter Ron Edwards stepped up, and said publicly, "There is nothing different about this other than the name of the victim."

Eventually, video from the ambulance circulated that allegedly showed something of substance, and even Minnesota Governor Mark Dayton commented on it. He advised media that he had seen the tape, but he could not reach any conclusions one way or the other. Practically everybody knew that had body cams been utilized, there would be no ambiguity as to what happened.

County Attorney Freeman eventually decided to ice the grand jury and make the charge decision regarding the two officers on his own. On March 30, 2016, he cleared the two officers citing a primary reason that the investigation concluded that the suspect's DNA was on an officer's gun. It was additionally determined that Clark was not cuffed.

The African-American community was clearly not satisfied, and as time went on, it seemed that most people of color in Minneapolis and also white people rejected Freeman's conclusions. A later civil lawsuit settled in 2020.

119

As part of the investigation, both of the officers had apparently supported this contention: An officer's gun was put up to Clark's mouth, and Clark was told to let go of the weapon, or he would be shot. One officer said Clark looked at him and said: "I am ready to die."

At the presser announcing the decision, Freeman was asked about that. As reported in a *Strib* article, Freeman said, "The only people who heard Jamar were the two officers and Mr. Clark, and he is not here." That was the problem with a dead citizen. He could not give his version – and neither could Terrance Franklin in May of 2013.

The problem with the Clark case from the beginning was that there was no video of substance. The Clark matter was another factor that led to a sharp push for body cams for field cops.

Our legal team, like many citizens, was at a point that without a video, we did not believe the contentions of law enforcement when it came to the shooting of citizens. This concept would especially come up with the killing of Justine Damond in 2017. We also saw something else that caught our eye: one of the MPD officers in Clark was represented by Fred Bruno. On Clark, Bruno clearly had done his job – and done it well. Without video, and a questionable police killing, his job was a lot easier.

During this time frame in the early developments of the Clark matter, news came out of Chicago, Illinois about the killing of a 17-year-old black male named Laquan McDonald. The killing took place on October 20, 2014, but substantive video depicting the event did not come out publicly until the end of November in 2015. Why did it take so long? The shooter was Jason Van Dyke, an officer with the Chicago Police Department (CPD). The story developed like this: Chicago quickly settled the matter before the filing of a lawsuit, but then an aggressive reporter sued under the Freedom of Information Act to secure video footage with the intuitive belief that what would be depicted would be really bad.

After a great deal of legal machinations, a judge in Chicago ordered release of the video. The key clip showed McDonald walking down a Chicago street allegedly holding a knife, and he is then shot 18 times with the officer far away not even in sight of the dash cam. The officer in question, Van Dyke, was charged with murder soon thereafter.

A political firestorm evolved. A few days after the video was released, Chicago Mayor Rahm Emanuel, who was already in hot water for a lack of transparency, fired Chicago Police Superintendent Garry McCarthy, Chicago's equivalent of a police chief. It was perceived that Emanuel and McCarthy had not done enough to institute reforms in CPD. Whether that was true or not, there were massive protests, and the video and media stories spread like wildfire throughout the nation.

Reporter John Kass, in an opinion piece for The *Chicago Tribune* on December 3, 2015, pointed out why there was a delay in releasing the video: Emanuel would not have been re-elected in November of 2014. This was a mayor who was considered to be invulnerable, and his entire tenure as mayor of one of the largest cities in the country was going up in flames, not to mention the head cop for CPD, all because of a single, relatively short dash cam video. The reality was that it took a year to indict an officer who shot a teenager 18 times for no good reason. It could be seen in the video that the officer was not in harm's way when he killed the black teenager.

This issue also came up: Did other officers assist Van Dyke with getting away with it? Reports of the incident by many officers were in complete contradiction with the dash-cam footage. The reports made it seem that McDonald was attacking them with a knife. There was also speculation that officers walked into a nearby Burger King ostensibly to secure restaurant video that may have picked up the event. The allegation was there was no plan to put the seized video into evidence. Officers protecting an illegal police officer shooter? Our team felt it sounded like a case from Minnesota with the last name "Franklin."

The sorry episode played its way out with, for example, Mayor Emanuel apologizing and vowing reform on December 9, 2015. African Americans were not buying it. Emanuel had an impressive career and was director of finance for Bill Clinton's campaign in 1992. He was in Congress from 2003 to 2009, and in 2008, he accepted the position of White House Chief of Staff for newly elected president, Barack Obama. He was elected Chicago mayor in 2010 and served two terms. Therefore, the contention of Kass that Emanuel may not have been re-elected was a reasonable contention since the vote for his second term would have been in November of 2014. McDonald was killed the month before.

Emanuel contended he was moving on to bigger things when he decided not to run again in 2018, but the common consensus was that his chance of re-election was slim to none, all because of a video that depicted a police officer, compensated by the City of Chicago taxpayers, illegally killing a young black male. The thought that occurred to folks in Chicago was how many other illegal killings of young black males by police had taken place where there was no video? Without the video, the false story of Van Dyke and other Chicago cops as depicted in so-called official reports would have gone down as the true story, and nobody outside of that small group of cops would have known any better. It was easy to see as the evidence slowly evolved that there was a major league cover-up beginning on the day McDonald was killed.

It was another black mark for American law enforcement that most certainly changed the perception of not only folks in Illinois, but nationwide. In 2018, Van Dyke was convicted of second-degree murder by a jury in Chicago. There was a separate trial against CPD officers alleging conduct to support a cover-up. They were acquitted in a bench trial – trial by judge, not jury. Many citizens in Chicago and nationwide did not accept this verdict.

The inevitable in the Terrance Franklin case then happened. On June 1, 2016, via courier, I received Sara Lathrop's motion for summary judgment scheduling a hearing date for September 2, 2016 before Judge Frank in St. Paul. The brief or memorandum of law was 42 pages with a total of 18 of the discovery deposition transcripts included, along with various police reports, and other items such as photographs. It was massive.

In addition to Sara, three other Assistant City Attorneys were listed on the pleadings. "Declarations," like affidavits, sworn statements under oath, were submitted for two of the attorneys to lay foundation for the exhibits/evidence.

The three-page introduction basically laid out their argument that the scenario of the SWAT basement cops was valid, there was no admissible evidence of use of the N-word, and that there was no evidence that Franklin had been killed after he had surrendered. It asked the judge to dismiss the case with prejudice based primarily on different forms of immunity.

Their detailed facts section of 10 pages basically articulated the story from the perspective of Stender, Meath, Peterson, Muro, and Durand. It then transitioned to the investigation of Kjos and Porras.

The brief did not ignore the Gaines' video clip, but other than pointing out the conclusions that Ed Primeau reached about the words that could be heard, they concentrated on the notion that this sound expert did not hear the N-word. They noted nothing about the significance of the words that could be heard including the fact that those articulated by Terrance alone was a complete contradiction to the version of the SWAT basement team. That was their only point: no N-word. Nothing about how those other words explained what happened in that basement. They went on to note that no case witness inside or outside of the Bickal home heard those words. We did not dispute that. The video spoke for itself.

All of this argument was interesting because we were convinced the defense team would absolutely object to anything Ed claimed he heard at the time of trial because it would invade the province of the jury. So this was, in essence, a legal version of wanting to have your cake and eat it too.

Then there was this gem: "Likewise, a review of the Gaines' video reveals that no reasonable juror could conclude that any audible voices could have been coming from the basement." What was strange about this argument was that the defense wanted the judge to accept some of Ed's conclusions but not all of them. Ed had already concluded that sounds could have come from the basement, and this conclusion was going to go into evidence. There was nothing our opponent could do about that.

As expected, the brief went on to allege that the "officers' actions were objectively reasonable," with citations to federal case law, and the officers were entitled to "qualified and official immunity."

Amazingly, the defense lawyers, in support of their contention this wrongful death claim should be dismissed, alleged that no wrongful act or omission could be pointed to that caused Terrance's death. Support for this was their version of the facts.

It is important to note that a federal judge, when addressing this type of motion, has to determine the facts in a light most favorable to the plaintiff, our client. So any version, as long as it is supported by competent evidence, and the Gaines' video clip alone fell into that category, would defeat the motion. We would then proceed to trial where the defendants would have to deal with the high risk of what a jury could do.

That was pretty much it. The defense brief said nothing about the words from Gaines' video, which provided a perfectly rational scenario about apprehension and officer anger. There was nothing about the significance of DOC Dave being handed the MP5 at the scene to explain the Franklin DNA. There was nothing about the significance of no blood being on the MP5. There was nothing about the time gap supported even by one of their own personnel, Officer Sporny. There was nothing about the incompetent, incomplete investigation, and on and on. We would make sure the judge knew about these matters with our response.

We submitted our response on July 8, 2016. Our brief, entitled "Plaintiff's Memorandum of Law in Opposition to Motion for Summary Judgment," was 25 pages in length. We submitted some depositions and other evidence our opponent had not, but their submissions did contain most of the key evidence in the form of the substantive depositions for the case.

Judge Donovan Frank was a former prosecutor from Duluth, Minnesota, a harbor town located approximately two hours from St. Paul right on Lake Superior. He was an appointee of former Senator Paul Wellstone who had passed away in a plane crash in October of 2002. I was one of the attorneys involved in the litigation from that crash.

As a Wellstone appointee, Judge Frank had the label of being a liberal judge. In my experience with him, however, I found him to be objective, intelligent, and not biased in any way. It was certainly true that some federal judges did not like claims against law enforcement, and drawing a judge with this mindset, which is completely at random, can be a problem. The bottom line with Judge Frank was that if we did not have viable evidence to defeat the defense immunity motion, our case would be dismissed forever, and short of a successful appeal with the Eighth Circuit Court of Appeals based out of St. Louis, Missouri, we would be in big trouble. There was a tendency for appellate courts to affirm federal judges who had dismissed 1983 claims for the reason of immunity. As such, we knew this was an incredibly important motion, and we therefore had to play all of our cards.

We broke down our approach to contesting this motion into four parts: (1) The initial attempted apprehension; (2) The Gaines' video as it tied into the time gap; (3) What occurred in the basement, i.e., whether Terrance shot a police firearm; and (4) How it was that Terrance's DNA innocently ended up on the MP5.

In addition to the Gaines' video, we submitted the apartment video for the court's review and alleged that Sergeant Smulski's contention that Terrance tried to injure or kill her was flat out false. The confusion with her recall and Sergeant Moore's was detailed including what supposedly went out over the police airwaves. I noted the fact that Moore testified that he never conveyed over police radio that the suspect attempted to injure or kill anyone.

We noted that DOC Dave, after viewing the video, admitted that Smulski was out of the way of the PT Cruiser Terrance was operating when that vehicle exited the apartment parking lot. Under oath, Dave actually said: "I wasn't aware of that."

Moore's mistake was highlighted that Smulski "jumped out of the way" and then his admission that it was the video that made him realize the mistake.

We pointed out to the court that it was these mistakes that led to the feeding frenzy and Terrance's ultimate death. I specifically noted in the brief that: "Defendants . . . had to have viewed Terrance as an attempted cop killer."

The time gap from the Gaines' video coupled with Officer Wyatt's testimony was detailed for the court with the support of experts Primeau and Harrington. We alleged a gap of 72 seconds from MP5 accidental discharge to the killing of Terrance.

Based on the words on the Gaines' video, we noted for the court the reasonable scenario of what happened in the basement as detailed in an earlier chapter.

In response to the defense contention that the N-word was never uttered by the 5-member SWAT team, we lobbed a grenade referring to the Green Bay incident. We also pointed out the huge discrepancy of the cops alleging that Terrance never spoke a word during the confrontation versus the fact that his voice could be heard on the Gaines' video in two separate places.

In the third section of the argument, I started like this:

The Defendant City and MPD circled the wagons after the events of 5/10/13 due in part to not only the not credible contention as to how Terrance Franklin died, but also the fact that an MPD officer coming to the scene long after Franklin was dead proceeded through a red light killing a citizen on a motorcycle. It is interesting that the MPD proceeded with this investigation on its own. Common sense cried out for an outside agency . . .

Obviously, we were aggressive and had to be. We wanted Judge Frank to promptly reject this motion on the merits. I emphasize the botched, weak investigation and the fact that the homicide investigators never engaged in any effort to enhance the Gaines' audio, which revealed the gunshots at second 53.

I then highlighted the testimony of each member of the SWAT team. We embraced what they said because it supported our case. Regarding Muro, I pointed out that he had no idea how he was shot. Mention was made of the fact that Muro heard over the SWAT van radio that the suspect tried to run over an officer with his car, and I also noted the closed laundry room door issue by stating for the court: "There was no rational reason for that door to be closed other than the notion that it was a discreet way to kill Franklin without others being able to see it."

For Meath, I noted the fact that he had no idea how he was shot, and his allegation that Terrance never spoke, a significant contradiction from the Gaines' video. Meath additionally could give no time estimate from the MP5 discharge to his killing of the suspect.

For Durand, I noted the handing of the MP5 to DOC Dave after the Franklin killing, and his inculpatory comments including to Sergeant Strauss that it was his gun in essence that was responsible for the situation. Durand additionally could give no estimate on the time gap.

126

I of course pointed out the lack of blood on the MP5 as discovered and reported by FS Kristen Jacobson. As such, I asserted the simple, basic contention that Durand could not have been in the laundry room when Terrance was killed.

For Stender, two points were made: The laundry room door was closed when Terrance was killed, and his vicious, immediate assault of Terrance with his fist and flashlight.

Regarding Peterson, I noted like the others (other than Durand), that he also had no idea how the MP5 discharged. His testimony that the time gap was only "a matter of seconds" represented another major discrepancy from the Gaines' video. The point Peterson made about the massive amount of blood in the laundry room was detailed for the court, a not surprising fact considering the large number of rounds that entered the head and neck region. The point for this was the lack of blood on the MP5, which was with Durand during the entire event because of the harness. I felt confident Judge Frank would consider this significant.

Lastly, I highlighted for the court the innocent explanation as to how Terrance's DNA ended up on the gun, DOC Dave's specious testimony that he was wearing gloves, and the additional fact that Dave's DNA was on the MP5 also.

I cited a great deal of case law alleging for the court that immunity was not applicable under these facts and, overall, that there were numerous factual issues such that summary judgment was not appropriate. We put together a strong, well-worded brief. We were confident that we would prevail on what we felt was a weak defense motion.

The oral argument for the motion took place on September 3, 2016, in Judge Frank's St. Paul courtroom. The lawyers basically repeated the points made in their briefs. Generally, the purpose of this type of hearing is merely to permit the judge to ask questions. In fact, the lawyers are not permitted to argue any law not contained within the briefs.

The only real highlight was that Judge Frank asked me this question: "You're basically claiming this is a murder, correct?"

"That's correct, Your Honor."

I felt why beat around the bush. If it was a murder, it was excessive force and therefore a wrongful death.

Federal judges do not have a time limit for rendering a decision on this type of motion, but we expected a decision within three months. We felt that the main thrust of our case would survive, and we would proceed to trial. We expected a trial date in perhaps six months once Judge Frank rendered his decision. We were wrong. Our opponent had other plans. But while we were waiting for that decision, a terrible event regarding the death of a black male at the hands of a police officer would happen right in the Twin Cities. It would garner national attention and sadly would result in the multiple murders of police officers in two different U.S. cities.

Chapter Twelve
Phil, Jennifer, and Justine

We filed our opposition motion papers for the case on July 8, 2016. Two days before, on July 6, a 32-year-old black man named Philando Castile was shot multiple times by a 28-year-old police officer during a traffic stop on Larpenteur Avenue in Falcon Heights, a small suburb northwest of St. Paul. I knew this would be ugly, and that thought quickly proved to be true.

Dash-cam video picked up much of what happened. The police officer, Jeronimo Yanez, was Hispanic and employed with the City of St. Anthony, a suburb just east of the Minneapolis border. He was not wearing a body cam. Castile's girlfriend, Diamond Reynolds, who was seated next to Castile in the front passenger seat, began to live stream video on Facebook right after it happened. To make matters worse, Diamond's daughter, only four years old, was seated in the back seat and was almost hit by a stray round.

The immediate aftermath images were brutal. Castile as the driver was pulled over merely for a mechanical issue. He told the officer he had a gun-carry permit and was armed. As he reached for identification at the officer's request, Yanez overreacted and shot Castile seven times. Castile was still alive for several minutes during the live stream but soon died at the scene. The whole situation was unbelievably sad.

This tragic news was covered by media instantly. The media, doing their due diligence, learned that Castile, known by his friends as "Phil," was a good man who worked in food service at a local elementary school. He had no criminal record to speak of other than various minor moving violations. Yanez claimed Castile's nose matched that of a burglary suspect. It came out later that Castile had been pulled over more than twenty times for minor traffic infractions.

Diamond's live stream went viral, and soon, the sad event was all over national news. It affected some folks differently including a man named Micah Johnson in Dallas, Texas. Apparently, this black male, an army reserve Afghan war vet, who was very proficient with firearms, including scoped assault rifles, could not take it any more with what he perceived as endemic racism in America. During a peaceful Black Lives Matter protest in downtown Dallas, one day after Phil was killed, and also the result of a recent police killing of a citizen in Baton Rouge, Louisiana, Johnson fired multiple rounds with various firearms. He shot from a parking ramp killing five Dallas police officers and injuring nine more. Johnson was subsequently found and killed that evening.

A few days later, President and Michelle Obama, along with Vice-President Joe Biden and his wife, Dr. Jill Biden, and former President George W. Bush and the former first lady, Laura Bush, appeared at a memorial in Dallas as a result of the tragedy. The entire country was in grief, not just for the unjust loss of life in Dallas, but also from what was perceived as an unjust killing of an African-American man in Minnesota by a young officer who just flat out panicked.

Why was all of this happening? The dash-cam video from the Yanez squad would not become public until after the Yanez criminal trial. Diamond, who became my client in 2017, was thrust into the public spotlight through no fault of her own for a guttural reaction to live stream, in her mind, to save her life and her daughter's life. This was because of a police officer who she correctly perceived seemed to have lost his mind in a moment of utter stupidity. It was video again. Video. This time in the form of a live stream by a young woman who reacted in that way to save her life. It was another example of how video was changing the American public's perception of police officers regardless of how the Castile case played out in courtrooms.

The tragedy did not end in Dallas. On July 16, 2016, ten days after Phil was killed, a black man named Gavin Long shot six police officers in Baton Rouge. Of the six shot, three died. Long, like Johnson in Dallas, was killed at the scene. This man was apparently connected to black separatist organizations, and it appeared his murderous rampage was a direct result of the killing of Phil in Minnesota and the day-before killing of a black man named Alton Sterling in Baton Rouge. Sterling was in a struggle with two officers when killed. No doubt Johnson had seen the video of Diamond's live stream and the Sterling killing – which was also depicted on citizen/bystander video.

130

Phil's case would proceed to play out in court. His family and Diamond certainly wanted justice, but nothing was going to bring him back. In November of 2016, Yanez was charged with second degree manslaughter and two counts of dangerous discharge of a firearm by Ramsey County Attorney, John Choi. It easily could have been worse for Yanez. It was hard to believe, but Choi's decision was such that he became the first county attorney in Minnesota history to bring criminal charges against a police officer involved in an on-duty fatal shooting. Was it any wonder Mike Freeman had decided not to file charges for the Franklin matter in 2013?

The world was changing. It seemed clear Choi's charges never would have happened without Diamond's video. It is worth repeating that Yanez had no body cam, and the moments right before he killed Phil were presumably not depicted well by the dash cam.

The news of the Yanez criminal charges came just at the time we received good news for our client, Walt Franklin. On November 10, 2016, Judge Frank issued his opinion regarding the defense motion for summary judgment argued in September. Regarding counts 1 and 2, plaintiff's claims under 42 U.S.C. § 1983 and the separate wrongful death claim, the defense motions to dismiss were denied. We had prevailed on the gravamen/main points of the case, and those claims would proceed to trial.

Judge Frank's reasoning was interesting. He placed emphasis on what we focused on. He noted on page 10 of his Memorandum Opinion and Order: "Considering all evidence in the record – including the Gaines' video and the Primeau report – the Court concludes that genuine issues of material fact preclude summary judgment as to the reasonableness of the force used against Franklin." We had achieved our goal.

Regarding Peterson and Meath, the judge went on to note: "While it is certainly true that officers Peterson and Meath were faced with a situation that posed a significant threat of death or serious physical injury to them or others, a factual dispute exists over whether such a situation was present at the time when the officers used deadly force against Franklin. Therefore, taking all facts in a light most favorable for plaintiff, the Court cannot conclude that qualified immunity shields Defendants." We felt that Judge Frank rejected the nonsensical story of the two cops.

Regarding the wrongful death claim, Judge Frank noted that "genuine factual disputes" existed regarding the defense-alleged sequence of events. As such, Judge Frank noted, "Factual disputes preclude summary judgment as to Plaintiff's wrongful death claim." The court additionally opined that the factual disputes prevented defendants from securing summary judgment for the issue of official immunity.

So now we thought we would have a trial date with Judge Frank in St. Paul federal court in the summer of 2017. Our opponent had other plans. Even though the case had yet to be determined on the merits, they had the right, and exercised that right, to proceed with an appeal, known as an "interlocutory appeal," to the Eighth Circuit Court of Appeals. Their goal was to have Judge Frank's decision reviewed and reversed. The date of this appeal intent was December 6, 2016 with the filing of a document called "Notice of Appeal." This legal maneuver would delay the trial of the case for at least two years, maybe even three. Our team felt the purpose of this was delay, nothing else. Nonetheless, we felt we would prevail on appeal also. But in the meantime, many events out of our control would happen – and help Walt and our team.

As the Yanez criminal case progressed, it was determined that the trial would take place at the end of June in 2017. There were various legal maneuvers for the high-profile case including a motion for change of venue that was denied by Judge William Leary III. The trial would be right in downtown St. Paul at the Ramsey County Courthouse.

I participated in a pretrial prep session for Diamond about a month before the trial, but on the day she testified, I let my associate Karlowba Powell handle that. It was an emotional day for Diamond. On direct, she said this in response to why she live streamed: "Because I know that people are not protected against the police, and I wanted to make sure that if I were to die in front of my daughter, people would know the truth." This had become the sad reality for African Americans in the United States. And as time went on, even white people who did not understand before were now getting it. Those not sympathetic to the black cause were coming around, I contend, primarily because of the technology of video. Even though Yanez did not have a body cam, it was easy to fill in the blanks of what happened just before Phil was shot. Phil was compliant. This was a young officer who made a terrible mistake, and then in my and Choi's opinion committed a crime by killing Phil for no good reason.

Every day of trial, the coverage was page-one news in both the *Pioneer Press* and *Star Tribune*. It was the lead story also on all of the Twin City television news stations. The courtroom was packed with media including reps from all over the country like the *Washington Post* and the *New York Times*. The courtroom atmosphere was palpably intense as I discovered when I attended the trial to hear Yanez testify and also for the closing arguments. What made matters worse was that the courtroom chosen for the trial was not the largest in the courthouse, and everyone was packed in like sardines.

I did not find Yanez credible when he testified but, unfortunately, the cross examination conducted by one of the three prosecutors was weak in my opinion. Overall, I was not impressed by the prosecution team. They just did not seem real motivated, and perhaps this was a factor to explain why after multiple days of deliberation, the St. Paul jury found Yanez not guilty on all counts. Prosecutors were usually beholden to law enforcement, and that was the case with these three from my perspective.

I felt the decision was an injustice, and it clearly exacerbated tensions in the Twin Cities and added to the boiling kettle that finally overflowed days after the George Floyd killing in May of 2020. The bottom line is that people had just had it with what seemed like continual injustice, and one of the highlights of this injustice was this absurd Yanez verdict. The reality is that Yanez should have been tried for third degree murder, and he could and should have been convicted of that charge and been incarcerated for years. If the Castile killing happened four years later, that would have been the result. Nonetheless, at least a conviction for manslaughter would have been just.

After the verdict, I was quoted in the *New York Times*. I could not hide my disappointment. Mitch Smith, an excellent reporter for the *Times*, identified me as Diamond's attorney and asked my thoughts. I said, "For those who are committed to the idea of leveling the playing field with law enforcement and the citizenry, it's a big blow."

Then, what made matters worse, evidence that the public had not seen was released, including the dash-cam video, which further exacerbated tensions. There were multiple demonstrations, and some got violent. After Phil's killing the absurd cops at the scene actually had the audacity to handcuff Diamond and put her and her daughter in the back of a police squad. That video also went viral. It revealed Diamond crying, and her darling daughter trying to calm her down. The image was so poignant that it became one of the most important seminal images in U.S. history to depict the struggle of black America against American law enforcement.

The interchange with Diamond was a tearjerker. This wonderful little girl, who became everyone's hero, said: "Mom, please stop cussing and screaming cause I don't want you to get shooted."

Diamond says, "Okay. Give me a kiss. My phone just died. That's all."

"I can keep you safe," the little hero says.

The employer for Yanez was not impressed with the verdict. The City of St. Anthony could not wait to hand Yanez a pink slip, and immediately, he was fired. He actually received a severance package of $48,000. Then, the heirs of Phil settled for $3 million with St. Anthony. Had that been a few years later, it would have been $20 million. Since Diamond was not married to Phil, she received nothing from this, but in November, she obtained a settlement for her and her daughter grounded in the legal theory of "zone of danger" for $800,000.

The weird happenings around us continued. Like clockwork, another bizarre situation occurred with the Minneapolis Police Department right after the dust settled from Yanez. For years, MPD officers had been shooting dogs in North Minneapolis, a section of Minneapolis whose citizens were primarily of color. On the night of July 8, 2017, a daughter of homeowner Jennifer LeMay failed to properly disengage the home's security alarm. Two MPD officers came to the scene, and rather than ascertaining with Jennifer's daughter that it was a false alarm, one of the officers, Michael Mays, scaled a backyard fence. One of the two dogs, a white dog named Ciroc, approached Mays wagging its tail. Mays backed up and then began shooting the dog. Clearly, in reaction to hearing its companion yelp, a second dog, Rocko, ran out of the house toward Ciroc and what was going on. Mays shot that dog too. Both dogs survived but were badly injured.

Mays proceeded to prepare a report that claimed that the two dogs charged him and, in essence, he had no choice but to shoot both. There was one rather large problem for Officer Mays: A surveillance camera on the outside rear of the home depicted the entire incident significantly contradicting his bogus report.

As one can imagine, owner Jennifer LeMay was beyond off-the-chart angry. I was retained. Jennifer had already posted the video on Facebook, and it went viral. I have been told by members of media that the house video, and the subsequent body-cam video, are the most watched videos of the shooting of dogs by a member of law enforcement in U.S. history.

We were able to promptly secure Mays' report. It was laughable for its inaccuracy – reminding one years later of the nonsense that came out about George Floyd – that he passed away due to "a medical emergency." It was amazing that this officer would be dishonest in light of the fact that he was wearing and had activated his body cam. He issued his "public data" report before he knew the home had competent surveillance video. The report had this language: "While staging at the rear, two large size pit bulls charged at officer. Officer dispatched the two dogs . . ." This was not the truth at all.

The dogs were actually purebred American Staffordshire Terriers. The use by some of the term "pit bull" had a negative connotation. The dogs were trained as emotional support dogs for health support: Ciroc – mental health and emotional support, and Rocko – seizure alert for pseudo seizures. They were my K-9 clients. They are beautiful, intelligent, loving dogs whose only negative is that they would try to lick me to death when I would go see them.

Surprisingly, the Police Officers Federation of Minneapolis, MPD's union, chimed in. Their position was that it was okay for the officer to shoot the dogs. When it came to the MPD police union, especially in controversial situations, a lack of objectivity could almost always be counted upon.

135

The LeMay case was garnering huge media attention, even nationwide, and although the home video was of good quality, what I wanted, and immediately, was the video of Mays' body cam. I decided to take a chance. I would reach out to Chief Harteau directly. With a letter dated July 12, 2017, I laid out the basic facts and asked in a kind way for release of the body-cam video. She cooperated. A representative of MPD contacted me almost immediately, and I had the video within a week. It was understood that we would disseminate it publicly, which we did. The public's response to the body-cam video was one of almost universal, unanimous outrage. The perspective with the body cam was better than the home video, and it was interesting to watch and hear the officer leave the backyard, scale the fence, and then head around to the front of the home to dialogue with Jennifer's daughter who was understandably distraught and crying.

Strangely, this type of technology, at least at the time, operated in such a way that the audio did not kick in for a minute. Mays made the not credible contention that when Ciroc first approached him, wagging his tail, he growled. Jennifer saw the video and based on her knowledge of her dog and its demeanor alleged this contention was complete nonsense. The point was, even without audio, this officer was able to engage in a false audio narrative, which would now be a matter for a jury to decide. And in that regard, I commenced suit with my co-counsel Devon Jacob out of Pennsylvania in September of 2019. Devon would later be on the team of lawyers for George Floyd. The LeMay case is not over. As of this date, to our knowledge, Mays has never been disciplined for his conduct.

Betsy Hodges was a member of the Democratic-Farmer-Labor Party (DFL), and after a term of 8 years on the Minneapolis City Council, became mayor of Minneapolis on January 2, 2014, succeeding R.T. Rybak. It was no surprise she was with the DFL. That party and the so-called Progressive movement had controlled Minneapolis for at least 50 years. She would serve only one term as mayor, and the reason why had to do primarily with another MPD officer shooting of a citizen.

As her position as mayor evolved, she would inherit the Franklin case for a time, but the political make-up of Minneapolis was such that the City Council really was in control of whether an excessive force case would settle or proceed to trial. There would be turbulent times for her including with the police chief she had inherited from her predecessor, Chief Janeé Harteau.

Reporters Erin Golden and Glen Stubbe of the *Strib* reported of the turbulence in an excellent page-one piece on January 2, 2016. In December, 60 citizens spoke at the Council's final budget hearing, and the mayor was their target. The contention was that city government was ineffective, out of touch, and racist. This message was interesting since the DFL had always been perceived as anything but.

The Hodges' campaign had been predicated on the notion of discontinuing inequities in education, employment, housing, and the justice system. The story made it seem that the Jamar Clark matter at the end of December was preventing her from moving toward her goals. One attendee asked her: "I want to ask you, mayor. Are you going to resign?"

Regarding Clark, the story noted that as "the protests and police pushback flared up, Hodges was criticized for not doing enough public communication." Protestors even showed up at her home. It was told to me during that time that members of MPD were livid at her for allowing the protesters to camp outside of the 4th Precinct for weeks. In short, it seemed everyone was mad at her, a toxic cocktail for any politician.

For the next year, things did not seem to improve when a public dispute evolved with her and the chief. Harteau wanted to promote Lieutenant John Delmonico, the former head of the police union and a controversial figure, to inspector of the 4th Precinct. The mayor allegedly learned of the plan only 90 minutes before the announcement. *Strib* Reporters Adam Belz and Dave Chanen, accessing anonymous sources, learned the mayor asked the chief to her office to discuss the matter in an April 28, 2017 story. Strangely, Harteau declined the meeting.

It seemed from that point forward the chief's days were numbered. Hodges would just need a reason. The story noted the background to this were conflicts with both regarding race and policing. I felt this was another example of the incredible trickle down effect of video, false narratives by police personnel, and then a perception by citizens that politicians were not reigning in the police. And why were politicians dropping the ball? There was a belief

137

system that without the support of the police, a politician could not get elected, or perhaps more importantly, re-elected. The same cycle had played out this way in Chicago as a result of the Laquan McDonald tragedy – and a single dash-cam video. Both Hodges and Harteau declined interviews for the Belz/Chanen story.

But Harteau was not just getting pushback from the mayor. Activists and community organizers from the "North Side" were livid with Harteau's Delmonico choice. Reference was made to "Pointergate" when Delmonico accused the mayor of flashing gang signs while posing with a young black male. It seemed clear Hodges had a pathological hatred of Delmonico – and this is who Harteau wanted to promote?

For his part, Delmonico knew this public spat would prevent the planned promotion. Then the current union head, Bob Kroll, another controversial figure, made matters worse by jumping into the fray and criticizing the mayor. The story made clear Hodges had the authority to kibosh the planned promotion.

But then the Peyton-Place scenario continued to play out publicly. Belz and Chanen reported in another page-one story on April 29, 2017 that Hodges did not object to the promotion until after the news was announced, and Chief Harteau had text messages to prove it. The only reason the chief refused to meet the mayor was because she was celebrating her daughter's 18th birthday. The bottom line was that the texts revealed the mayor first backed the chief for Delmonico's promotion.

In the texts, not surprisingly, Hodges referred to the progressive community remembering that Delmonico had commented on Pointergate and that Delmonico in the past had said "racist stuff." It was equally obvious the texts had been handed to the press on a silver platter by Chief Harteau.

Hodges then issued a statement during this time frame, which said: "John Delmonico will not be the inspector of the 4th Precinct."

This was an ugly public mess that would be exacerbated with the shooting of Ciroc and Rocko. Paul Walsh ran a page-one Metro story that featured both dogs and Jennifer on July 11, 2017. The chief was quoted as saying, "It was hard to watch," but she did not criticize the officers.

But all hell was about to break loose, and it was all because of a single round fired from the gun of a Minneapolis police officer. Our legal team would dub it "Franklin #2."

It was all over the news beginning on July 17, 2017. A small page-one story appeared in the *Pioneer Press* on that Monday. The *Star Tribune* and television media were all over it too. As reported by *Pioneer Press* reporters Fred Melo and Nick Woltman, "A woman was shot to death late Saturday by police regarding a 911 call in South Minneapolis."

The story was cryptic and vague because MPD and the BCA were vague. Officers responded at 11:30 p.m. for a possible assault at the block of 5100 Washburn Avenue South. The BCA said, "One of the officers shot and killed the woman."

A man was identified, Zach Damond, as a son of the woman's fiancé. The woman had called the police after hearing a noise near her home. The story had this quote attributed to Zach: "My mom is dead because a police officer shot her for reasons I don't know. These cops need to get trained differently. I just know she heard a sound in the alley, so then she called the police, and the cops showed up . . . Next thing I know, they take my best friend's life." An MPD cop killed the 911 caller?

Mayor Hodges was already in the mix. Certainly, she knew this would be bad. "We have few facts at this point," she said. "This is an awful situation. My heart goes out to everyone in the community, especially the family of the woman who was shot."

Then there was this, as dutifully reported by Melo and Weltman: "The officers' body cameras were not turned on during the shooting, and the squad-car camera did not capture it," according to the BCA.

After reading that, I called my go-to Franklin investigator, Steve Rogers, and firearms' consultant, Alan Rogers. "It's false narrative time, guys," I said to them.

They both replied: "Yeppers."

The situation slowly played out in the media each day further angering the Minnesota citizenry. It would be bizarre and convoluted and when all told, would be a clear attempted cover-up.

The victim was a 40-year-old Caucasian woman, of Australian descent, named Justine Ruszczyk Damond. Amy Forliti of the

Associated Press provided details in her July 18, 2017 story, which was page one in the *Pioneer Press*. The meditation teacher was strangely killed by an MPD officer who fired from the passenger seat of his squad car. If that was the case, it would mean he shot across his partner. This made no sense – unless it was an accident.

The story confirmed Justine was the 911 caller. She believed a sexual assault had occurred in an alley near her home. So how would the 911 caller end up dead? The whole situation was crazy. Surely, it had to be an accident, and this was confirmed in my mind (all opinions in this section on the Damond matter are mine, not any member of my legal team) when it was learned the officer fired only one round. Officers who shoot to kill almost always fire more than one round.

Justine died of a single gunshot wound to the abdomen. Her fiancé, Don Damond, had been told essentially nothing by authorities. There were no witnesses other than the two officers. And the third person who presumably would have information of substance was dead.

Justine's Australian family was now in the mix and released a statement through that country's Department of Foreign Affairs as reported by Forliti: "They are trying to come to terms with this tragedy and to understand why this happened." It sounded as if every citizen of that country was in shock, and Justine, from Sydney, was engaged to be married to Don Damond in August.

It was now two days after her death, and no public explanation had been provided by MPD or the BCA. The BCA said more information would be disclosed once the officers were interviewed. The BCA - I knew right away that was a bad sign. They were beholden to Minnesota law enforcement, and that certainly included the Minneapolis Police Department.

Ruben Rosario, a well known excellent columnist for the *Pioneer Press*, spoke eloquently on what was going on in his column of July 18, 2017: "It certainly has not been a good month public-relations wise for Chief Janeé Harteau and the Mill City police force [MPD]. On July 8, a police officer shot a dog, reportedly a service pet, that . . . did not appear to be running or showing any hostile actions toward him . . . . Perhaps the key question other than why the cop fired at an unarmed woman is why neither officer in the squad car had their body cameras turned on." Rosario hit the nail on the head. That was what everyone was thinking – including me. But what about the squad video? That would probably tell much of the story with audio alone in the cab of the squad. Audio could be important like in Franklin.

Early on, my hypothesis was accidental discharge. The question then would be this: Would MPD engage in a cover-up like they did in Franklin?

Rosario noted that Mike Freeman would again make the charge decision himself. No grand jury.

Jon Tevlin, another excellent reporter for the *Strib,* commented on the sorry state of affairs in his column of July 19, 2017: "We are international news, again, for all the wrong reasons. It's no longer a surprise to see the folks you see on the nightly national news at the scene of suspicious, baffling deaths at the hands of our law enforcement officers." Tevlin cited Justine's Facebook page. He noted her "as a woman with an inordinate amount of humanity and optimism." He referenced a picture of Buddha, with a quote from Justine: "When you realize how perfect everything is, you will throw your head back and laugh at the sky."

So what was MPD and the BCA going to do? Go belly up and make clear this was an accident? Or start a false narrative with the potential behind-the-scenes involvement of the ever-available Federation attorney, one Fred Bruno, or someone else? I eventually concluded Bruno was not responsible for this false narrative.

Well, it began on July 19, 2017, as relayed by a Woltman *Pioneer Press* story. "The partner of the Minneapolis police officer who fatally shot Justine Damond . . . told investigators that he heard a loud noise near their squad . . . before the shooting." This was based on a news release by the Minnesota Bureau of Criminal Apprehension. The officer was identified as Matthew Harrity.

So the issue was this: Did the other officer, Mohamed Noor, who was Somali and black, develop fear such that he intentionally shot his gun to protect himself and his partner? It was soon learned that on the advice of counsel, Noor was not talking and would never give a statement to the authorities. His story would not come out until the time of his criminal trial long into the future.

But here was the problem with Harrity: Did he tell that story on the date of the incident? And was there technological evidence to back him up? All indicators were, based on early-on reports, that there was nothing to corroborate this. Was this a false narrative or was it legit? That would be the big question up until the eventual trial in April of 2019. But much would happen before then, most of it not good. For example, a big question was: Did the officers violate MPD policy by not having their body cams activated? Conveniently, the BCA was not investigating that. The fact Noor was not talking was a strong sign he would allege he fired intentionally rather than that it was an accidental shot.

Associated Press reporter Steve Karnowski noted in his July 20, 2017 column with Forliti that without Noor's version "there's virtually no explanation for what happened . . . when he fired a shot from the passenger seat of the squad . . . past his partner in the driver's seat . . . and killed Damond who was standing outside of the vehicle." The fact pattern could not be any stranger.

Chief Harteau then spoke as recorded in another page-one Associated Press story by Forliti and Karnowski on July 20, 2017. She said: "The actions in question go against who we are in the department . . . [they] should not have happened." She added: "This did not have to happen; Justine did not have to die."

I reached out to one of my law enforcement contacts. He told me that MPD officers had a tendency to pull their sidearm and "lap it" for certain calls. This person told me that an active rape call at night would fall in that category. From a trajectory perspective, if one lifted the gun a few inches, it would line up such that a shot from the passenger seat would go by the driver-seat partner, out the driver-seat window, and strike the victim, in this case, Justine, where it hit her outside of the squad. He believed, and I agreed, that it was clearly accidental or negligent discharge. Noor could have just as easily hit Harrity. The family had already hired heavy-hitter private attorney, Bob Bennett, for the wrongful death claim. The city could end up shelling out millions as a result of their self-insured status.

The *Strib* also had an on point page-one story the same day authored by Andy Mannix and Emma Nelson. Chief Harteau added that the body cams should have been turned on. More than anything, that is what the public was fixated on. A mistake could be understood – not the missed ability to record the mistake. It was back to the public's basic belief that if you have the technology, use it.

On July 24, Paul Walsh and Sarah Jarvis of the *Strib* noted the release of the body cams for the shooting of Jennifer's dogs by MPD Officer Mays. The seminal image of Mays as he is about to shoot Ciroc was displayed in the paper. Ciroc seems to be cowering right before he is shot.

The still image was remarkable and left no doubt that Mays was just another officer who panicked – like Yanez the summer before. Jennifer and I were quoted throughout the story. I referred to the Damond matter, and said there should be "no more excuses" for officers to not have their body cams activated.

Then the next day, a bombshell: Chief Harteau, who had arguably been our main nemesis in Franklin, abruptly resigned. Libor Jany, Mannix, and Eric Roper of the *Strib* had a large font, page-one story. The caption was: "Chief Harteau is Forced Out." The reason was "growing criticism from the public and City Council."

Mayor Hodges asked her to resign then nominated Assistant Chief Medario Arradondo, a black man and 28-year veteran of the force to replace her. Harteau had been chief for four and a half years. It seemed clear another factor with the chief's demise was fallout from the Damond killing. Hodges issued a statement that read in part, "I have lost confidence in the chief's ability to lead us further." Protesters had delayed the mayor's press conference, which was interrupted after it began. The whole situation was pretty much a fiasco.

It seemed Harteau was a scapegoat. Even Ron Edwards spoke in her defense and noted she was a good chief. But Bob Kroll, the MPD union head, was not shedding any tears. He described her as vengeful and not understanding of the needs of the rank and file. But Kroll, never one to curry favor, alleged Hodges pushed Harteau out for political reasons because it was an election year.

The public outrage over Damond, as voiced by the *Strib*'s Editorial Board, was the ambiguity as to why body cams were not on 24/7 by MPD cops in the field. The Board closed out its July 22, 2017 piece with a prophetic comment: " . . . we'll reserve final judgment on Noor until the case plays out." And how would it play out? In a case that appeared to be one of negligent discharge, our legal team was quite interested along with all of Minnesota.

More information was coming out especially about the conduct of the BCA as it pertained to the Noor investigation. Adam Belz reported in an August 15, 2017 *Strib* piece that the BCA went into Justine's home with a warrant looking for God knows what. Folks in Southwest Minneapolis were angered by the move, and it was unusual in the sense that it was an example of "investigators scouring the home of a person shot and killed by the police" as Belz noted. It was a picture of what was to come.

Amazingly, a little over two months after Justine was killed, an audit of MPD body-cam use revealed little progress with mandatory use as reported by the *Strib* Editorial Board on September 21, 2017. Many problems were detailed, and the Board made this reasonable point: "Citizens and taxpayers have a right to expect that body cameras that are issued will be used."

With situations like this, although I had some sources, our main way to get information was the *Strib*, a media entity which always seemed to have its finger on the pulse. We felt the Damond case, how it played out, could affect defense counsel in our case regarding possible settlement due to its parallels with Franklin. It was important to follow it closely – especially a possible criminal trial for Noor, which seemed inevitable. Mike Freeman had yet to make a charging decision, and it was four months since Justine had been killed. The bottom line was that it was important to monitor the Damond case closely, and I decided to handle that task myself.

An amazing development was revealed with a December 15, 2017 front-page story by *Strib* reporter Brandon Stahl. At a union event, Freeman was confronted by activists, and one had a recording device. He was asked understandably why it was taking so long to make a charging decision on Noor considering five months had gone by. He said, "Fair question. I've got to have the evidence, and I don't have it yet. Let me just say it's not my fault. So if it isn't my fault, who didn't do their job? Investigators. They don't work for me. They haven't done their job."

This was clearly a major criticism of the BCA, which I always felt when it came to investigating the police was next to worthless for one reason alone – conflict of interest. They worked closely with Minnesota law enforcement. It was that simple.

Freeman then said, almost cavalierly, regarding reaching a decision: "[It's] a big present I want under the Christmas tree." The Damond family, shocked by his comments, was "deeply distressed and unhappy" according to Bob Bennett, the attorney for the heirs.

This is how it had been for years. Those in charge in Minneapolis, and elsewhere in Minnesota, including the BCA, just did not take police wrongdoing seriously. Piece by piece it was events like this that added to the cauldron, and it boiled over starting two days after George Floyd was killed on May 25, 2020. How bad was it? It was the worst property damage from rioting in U.S. history, second only to Los Angeles after the 1992 not guilty verdict in the police beating of Rodney King. He survived. George Floyd did not.

The powers that be just sat back and complained rather than taking the investigation away from the BCA for the Damond matter. The BCA continued to stumble forward.

The BCA issued some lame comment that did not placate anyone. It did come out however, that the BCA turned the case over to Freeman on September 12, but he had asked for additional investigation. This is what he had told the activists who had recorded him on December 14. He treated the activists respectfully and asked them to have "patience."

The reality was getting the full story was never going to be possible because Noor was not talking – which was his right – but it resulted in his termination. On December 22, the *Strib* Editorial Board lashed out at Freeman calling his decision to comment on an active case "a troubling lapse of professional ethics." How things would change by May of 2020. The charging decision regarding George Floyd's death took days, not months. The Minnesota governor in 2017, Mark Dayton, even jumped into the fray and criticized Freeman and defended the BCA. In my purely intuitive opinion, most Minnesotans were not buying the governor's defense of the BCA. But the bottom line was this: Five months had gone by, and nothing was happening to charge Noor, conduct that at the very least called out for a manslaughter charge.

Time went on into January and February of 2018. Nothing. Then, on February 26, 2018, the *Strib* Editorial Board reported that MPD was still being pokey at the transition to body-cam usage for its field cops. There were more excuses from MPD. The contention was that only 2 percent of body-cam usage would be audited each quarter. The public was getting more and more angry.

It was then reported by Riham Feshir of MPR News that Freeman had convened a grand jury at the end of January 2018, which seemed unusual since he said he would make the charging decision himself. But it then actually made sense: Freeman was calling MPD cops to testify before the grand jury as an investigatory tool. Could it be MPD personnel had not cooperated with the BCA? I again smelled a cover-up.

Then, on March 2, 2018, *Strib* reporter Libor Jany reported more Peyton-Place news that was like the tiff the year before with Mayor Hodges and Chief Harteau: The MPD union head, Bob Kroll, was upset because Freeman had secured subpoenas on dozens of MPD personnel and threatened contempt of court if they did not cooperate.

This dynamic was interesting because any county attorney, like Mike Freeman, needed the cooperation of the local cops to successfully prosecute criminal cases. His team of lawyers, known as assistant county attorneys, had a close symbiotic relationship with MPD cops, detectives, etcetera, for obvious reasons. Now, MPD's union head was in a public brouhaha with the county attorney.

But what was perhaps most interesting was that MPD was not cooperating with Freeman, a man who was simply trying to figure out how an innocent citizen was killed by one of their guys. It was a slow evolution for me, but it was clear that Freeman was in fact doing his job and was not going to let anyone stop him. The bottom line was that Freeman was making smart decisions, and due to his leadership, the citizens of the state of Minnesota were ultimately going to receive a top-notch prosecution, which is exactly what they were entitled to.

Media interaction for a county attorney in a case like this is important, and Freeman was doing an excellent job with media also. His media relations guy was Chuck Laszewski. I had gotten to know Chuck years before when he was a reporter for the *Pioneer Press* and really liked him. He was smart, had a good sense of humor, and was a perfect representative for County Attorney Freeman with the reality of many high profile cases like Damond.

Kroll's whining was in really bad taste and was another reason that people as a whole had gotten to a point that when people like

146

Kroll and his predecessor, the monumentally never-objective John Delmonico, talked, people just did not listen. I respected Kroll, but his complaining in this scenario was way out of line. Freeman had a perfectly sensible response: "I'm a little disappointed – probably more than a little – about some of the pettiness that we're hearing from the Police Federation." But then, the cat was out of the bag. It was unbelievable. We learned that MPD personnel were in fact not cooperating.

Freeman's office had asked for voluntary statements, a normal course of conduct with investigations, and they had refused. And the blame was the Police Federation "or its lawyers." To me, that meant Fred Bruno again, but I was not sure.

Then, Freeman had this understandable assessment which shocked everyone in the Twin Cities, but not me: "I've been a prosecutor . . . 19 years. This is the first time that I've ever had to subpoena police officers to tell us what they know." MPD, it was clear, was hell bent on preventing the Hennepin County Attorney and, therefore, the public, from getting the truth about how an innocent woman and citizen, Justine Damond, died. It was really that simple – and really that despicable. We were right – this would be Franklin #2.

Then it happened: splashed all over print media and television news – and nationwide and world-wide news coverage on March 21, 2018: Freeman had made his decision: Mohamed Noor was charged with third degree murder and the lesser included offense of second degree manslaughter. Third degree murder had an interesting definition: causing the death of another person, without intent, but by perpetrating an act evincing a depraved mind. Those last three words would be fixated on by media and legal scholars for over a year up to the April, 2019 trial.

Details of the last moments of Justine Damond's life were disclosed by the media. The single shot by Noor was confirmed. Harrity and Noor arrived in a squad and saw no suspicious activity. They were ready to leave when Harrity was "spooked" by someone outside the police car as reported by Libor Jany in his page-one *Strib* story of March 21. Harrity said he "feared for his life." Apparently, an attractive blonde woman in a robe or pajamas, barefoot, had this man in fear. I found that contention absurd, and that issue would be hotly

147

litigated. The *Strib* had in large font: "Culpable Negligence" with a subtitle, "Murder, Manslaughter Charges for Ex-Cop Noor."

And there was this sad detail: Harrity heard Justine say, just before she passed away, "I'm dying," or "I'm dead."

Freeman went the path of least resistance and decided on the notion that Noor intentionally fired his gun. I did not believe that for a minute, but I did not blame Freeman for going that route. Freeman had to surmise - put the pieces together from others - since Noor had never given a statement. He probably concluded Noor would allege he intentionally shot. The honorable thing would have been for Noor to just plead guilty to manslaughter – admit the mistake. That was never going to happen here. Freeman said, " . . . officer Noor recklessly and intentionally fired his handgun from the passenger seat, a location at which he would have been less able than officer Harrity to see and hear events on the other side of the squad car." I certainly agreed with that.

As the matter progressed, Noor would post bond and be out of jail up to trial. He was represented by Peter Wold and Tom Plunkett. I had known Tom for years and liked him, but he had his hands full with this mess. A conviction seemed likely with the current posture on how citizens viewed police officers in 2019, not like 10 or even 5 years earlier. The changed perception was primarily because of video. The Noor case would not have video, but because of that, citizens, and the Noor jury, in my opinion would be less likely to believe police officers who did not have technology to back them up.

The trial began on April 10, 2019, before Hennepin County Judge, Kathryn Quaintance. She was a former prosecutor I knew well from prior cases. I liked, admired, and respected her. She was a fair, intelligent, and experienced judge who I felt was perfect for the case.

The lawyers from Freeman's office who would try the case were Pat Lofton and Amy Sweasy. I knew Pat some but had never tried a case with him. He was a tall man with a formidable presence in the courtroom. He had the classic demeanor of a prosecutor: tough and intelligent. Sweasy was unknown to me, but by the time the Noor case was over, I would conclude those two would conduct the best murder prosecution in state history. Their work could not have been better, and they were a great team. I learned from my sources early on

148

that they were chosen to prosecute the four MPD officers in the George Floyd killing, but then politics got in the way.

The seminal issue at the Noor trial would be this: Was the alleged loud sound supposedly caused by the victim Justine slapping the squad car, or was that a false narrative maybe created by a lawyer or someone else? Lofton and Sweasy did the right thing – they took it head on. If the jury believed the slap happened, it enhanced the possibility that the officers were in legitimate fear, and maybe the jurors would throw Noor a bone and find him not guilty. I for one never believed it from the beginning and felt it was a weak false narrative. But my opinion was meaningless. It came down to the jury.

Normally, if I comment on a trial, I prefer to have attended or at least read the trial transcript. With the trial of *State of Minnesota v. Mohamed Noor* in April of 2019, my schedule was such that there was no way I could attend what would be a multiple-week trial. However, I did have someone in the courtroom, who will go unnamed, who briefed me every day. In addition, the daily trial reports of *Strib* reporters Libor Jany and Chao Xiong were superb and the best I had ever seen for a high-profile murder case. With these resources, I felt confident I was getting the accurate story to determine its relevance to Franklin and comment about it to others, which included radio commentary before, during, and after the trial on Cory Hepola's morning radio show with WCCO Radio in Minneapolis. Like the Yanez case, there was media present from all over the country and from outside of the country including the U.K. and Australia.

Most of the trial was the State's case – presented by Lofton and Sweasy. The defense case was short – only an expert witness and the defendant, Noor. But in my opinion, the case really came down to three witnesses: Sergeant Shannon Barnette, Noor's partner Matthew Harrity, and Noor himself. But there were others that helped the State meet its burden of proof.

Like all jury trials, after the jury was selected with the assistance of the trial judge, Judge Quaintance, the attorneys began with their opening statements. Lofton handled this for the State. Argument is not permitted in openings. Lawyers usually speak in terms of what the evidence will show. Lofton alleged that neither Noor nor Harrity mentioned anything about any loud noise on the night of the event. He alleged there would be no believable evidence to support that the loud noise happened other than the statements of the two officers. In essence, both Lofton and Sweasy were claiming that it was made up to avoid criminal culpability. Noor's conduct in shooting Damond evinced a depraved mind for third degree murder. He never should have shot her.

Peter Wold handled the opening for the defense. He claimed Noor followed his training and had good reason to be on guard in the alley. Then, to recreate the sound his client alleged he heard, Wold slammed his right hand on a table loudly for dramatic effect. This, he claimed, prompted Noor to fire to protect his partner. He referred to the situation as a "classic ambush scenario" and a possible "set up." The loud sound and the overall situation prompted Noor to fire, Wold alleged.

The strategy of the prosecutors was interesting. They would call MPD personnel who normally are cooperative witnesses for the State's case. Here, however, the typical witness could be categorized as hostile, which would permit questions in cross-examination or leading mode. This could be established if an MPD witness did not voluntarily appear to give a statement and/or demanded a subpoena, as examples.

It was also extraordinary in the sense that MPD and the Hennepin County Attorney's Office were normally teammates to get criminal convictions. Here, there was clearly a hostile relationship since Freeman's prosecutors were trying to get a murder conviction of an MPD officer. Considering the history of these two entities, it was a very different dichotomy.

The first witness was Don Damond for "spark of life" testimony. In a Minnesota murder case, the State is permitted to call a witness to testify as to the victim's life, and her fiancé, Mr. Damond, certainly had foundation for that. He was in Las Vegas when he got the call from investigators about what had happened to Justine. He was in tears when he described having to call her parents in Australia to give them the bad news. He described it as the "worst phone call" he ever had to make.

Justine had taken his last name professionally before their marriage, which was scheduled in a month for August of 2017. Members of Justine's family were in the courtroom and cried also. As explained to me, it was probably the most poignant moment for the entire trial.

The theory of Lofton and Sweasy was a cover-up – a false narrative for what the officers claimed happened. A key witness for this topic was Sergeant Shannon Barnette who the prosecutors would call as a witness in their case and promptly established as a hostile witness. She had to be subpoenaed for the grand jury but voluntarily met twice with Noor's attorneys on her own. This alone established her bias. I felt that Barnette was the Noor version of Sergeant Katherine Smulski from Franklin.

Barnette was one of the first to arrive at the scene. After she arrived, she says to an officer, "I'm on." She then deactivates her body cam. Sweasy asked her why. Barnette said, "To let them know anything they say will be on my body camera."

When asked why she turned her body cam off, Barnette said she did not know. Her device was off for two minutes and six seconds – and then she turned it back on. When asked why, she said, "No idea."

She claimed the body-cam policy at the time was confusing. Her camera caught her conversation with Officer Harrity who said, "She just came out of nowhere. I had my gun out. I didn't fire. And then Noor pulled out and fired." This description supported what my police officer source had told me. Officers would lap their guns at times, a violation of department policy that would enhance the possibility of accidental discharge.

Barnette looked for Noor and turned her camera off again. The whole scenario made no sense except for this: Nothing about a slap or a loud noise was mentioned by anyone.

To supplement this, 5th Precinct Inspector Kathy Waite was called. She made clear she did not hear anything about a loud noise or slap that evening or anything about the notion that the two officers thought they were under ambush when Noor fired.

It was clear. The slap or loud sound was just made up. But who was responsible for this false narrative and when did it begin? That is what I wanted to know, and I had some thoughts.

More evidence was presented that revealed a circle-the-wagons scenario at the scene and then for days after. Who cared about the rights of this dead woman, her family, or her fiancé? What was more important it seemed was getting away with it, that is, somehow rationally explaining Noor's conduct.

This was like Franklin: a strange, hard to explain police killing, then strange happenings with the investigation, and then a bizarre, final, not credible conclusion subject to being picked apart – which was exactly what Lofton and Sweasy were doing. Their skills were admirable, but ultimately, although each side would call use-of-force experts, in my opinion, the case came down to the credibility of Harrity and Noor.

Officer Matthew Harrity would testify on April 18, 2019. He would be escorted to court by none other than his attorney, Fred Bruno. This was my first knowledge of Bruno's involvement in the case. Harrity testified as everyone expected he would: that he heard a "thump" and feared a possible ambush before his partner, Noor, shot and killed Justine.

After the shooting, Harrity's body cam was activated, and the last moments of Justine's life were picked up, gasping for air, as attempts were made to save her through CPR. I was told it was hard to watch. She was barefoot in pajamas.

There was no testimony from Harrity that Noor had extended his arm out to shoot. This of course supported accidental discharge, but the prosecutors were not trying to prove that.

Sweasy asked this big question: If Harrity was startled, why didn't he shoot? He claimed he did not have time to "analyze the threat." But he added that shooting would have been "premature." He had only been an officer for a year when the Damond killing happened.

What was perhaps most strange was that Barnette had testified that she had several conversations with Harrity after the shooting and spoke to him once at the scene. But Harrity said he never spoke to Barnette about the case. How could this be? This was not the type of subject, it seemed to me, where there could be an honest mistake. One of them had to be lying.

The State could not call Noor to testify. That would be in the defense case, but it was possible he would not testify. It should be noted that Chief Arradondo testified. He said, with no gray area, that the body cams of both officers should have been activated. It was refreshing to hear from an honest witness.

Lofton and Sweasy called two use-of-force experts on police tactics. They buried the defense. In so many words, they said that Noor's alleged fear was not enough to permit him to shoot and kill an innocent victim. Although the defense would call an expert to refute this, and one could argue that the experts cancelled themselves out, this evidence alone could result in Noor's conviction.

And then there was something else: An expert on fingerprints found 51 latent prints on the outside of the Harrity/Noor squad, and none matched Justine Damond.

This was the main problem with false narratives. It was almost impossible to keep the story straight and match it with other evidence of substance. If the truth was told, generally, everything would seem to fall into place. But not with dishonest stories. It was like with DOC Dave in Franklin. His claim that he had gloves on when he was handed the MP5 didn't match with the scientific evidence. If he had gloves on, there was no rational, competent explanation for how his DNA ended up all over the MP5.

The State's case ended on April 24, 2019. It took two weeks. It seemed clear Noor would testify – and he did – on April 25, 2019. At this time even before his testimony, and this would be the first time the public heard his version, I felt he was guilty of letting people convince him to articulate a false narrative with the alleged loud sound. I am not saying his lawyers were responsible for this. Who it was, I do not know as of this day. He was a young officer, only two years on the job, and he made a big mistake and accidentally fired his gun. It could have easily missed Justine, but sadly, fate had its way on the evening of July 15, 2017.

So the question one might ask of Noor is: Why not just admit that it was an accident? The problem was that admission would result in a felony conviction for manslaughter, and his career would be over. If he took a page out of the Yanez playbook, from a little less than two years before, he could possibly be found not guilty. In my opinion, this is exactly what happened. Utilize fear as a defense. And there was this: He could be perceived as a hero for protecting his partner. Yanez did not have that angle, but his jury bought it, and he was found not guilty.

Here was the problem for Noor: if it was an accident, he could apologize and probably end up with at most a year in jail. Since it was clear to Freeman, Lofton, and Sweasy he would say he intended to shoot Justine, third degree murder was the appropriate charge, but even with mitigating factors, he could easily end up with a prison sentence of over 10 years. A conviction on that charge could actually be as high as 25 years.

I was confident Noor let others make the decision for him. He was taken advantage of, I felt, and it was not necessarily the fault of his attorneys. After the opening statement of Peter Wold, it seemed there was no going back. The case actually could have still resolved at any stage of the process – even after the trial began. But now it was time for him to testify. Would the jury believe him? Based on what had already come into evidence, it certainly did not seem that the alleged loud-sound defense would sell.

Noor's testimony began on a Thursday afternoon, April 25, 2019, and he was on the stand for hours running into the next day. It seemed like everything in this case was taking longer than normal, and nobody really could be blamed.

Noor said they pulled up in an alley behind the Damond home. He said he heard a loud bang, and Harrity yelled, "Oh, Jesus!" He alleged Harrity turned to him with fear in his eyes and was not able to unholster his gun.

He claimed he saw a woman "raising her right hand." He then said, "I fired one shot. The threat was gone." The hero testimony came next: He fired because he was protecting his partner. He believed his partner feared for his life. Noor said his "world came crashing down" after he confirmed Justine was dead. That certainly could be understood.

But when a witness testifies, there is almost always cross examination, and surviving that is the trick. His claim he put his left hand on his partner's chest then extended his right hand to shoot was not supported by Harrity. That was problem #1. Then Sweasy really pressed him on his decision to fire. He admitted he did not see Justine's hands before shooting. That was problem #2.

Throughout, he kept repeating that Harrity feared for his life, but Harrity never said that. That was problem #3. He then concluded after he got out of his squad, Justine was not a threat. That was problem #4.

What police officer would intentionally shoot across his partner at a target? This was further evidence of accidental discharge, but Lofton and Sweasy were not trying to prove that. Path of least resistance was the way to go, and I understood that. Just go with the flow. If Noor said he intentionally shot her, that would be in the category of third-degree murder, and these facts fell in that category. Noor's lawyers were gambling that fear would sell like it did in Yanez.

Noor's testimony reminded me of Meath and Peterson from Franklin. They also, in so many words, portrayed themselves as heroes.

All that was left were the closing arguments. Sweasy's closing was basic and to the point. The 911 caller coming up to the squad should not have been a surprise to the officers. Noor had never said he saved his partner's life when discussing the shooting with others. Most importantly, she highlighted the differences with Harrity's version and Noor's. She said, "They both can't both be right." She alleged, quite correctly, that the officers at the scene were trying to figure out a good reason for the shooting. She said, "The silence started to set in."

Plunkett handled the defense closing. He repeated the slap on the table his co-counsel Wold used at the beginning of the trial. He repeated the defense: "An officer may use deadly force to protect themselves or others from apparent danger." At this point, that argument seemed to ring hollow and insincere. The jury would now have the case.

The jury began their deliberations on Monday, April 29, 2019. After about a day of deliberations, a unanimous verdict was rendered on April 30. Noor was found guilty of third-degree murder and second-degree manslaughter. He was taken away in handcuffs. Sentencing was set for June 7.

Just a few days later, on May 3, it was disclosed that the City of Minneapolis had settled with Justine's family for $20 million. No prior death case caused at the hands of a Minnesota police officer, MPD or otherwise, had ever settled for close to that figure.

Judge Quaintance had no sympathy. On June 7, 2019, she sentenced Noor to 12 ½ years of prison. With good time, he would serve two-thirds of that. She said: "The law does not allow leniency because someone is a good person."

The Noor saga was over. It was my belief that if Noor had told the truth that the shooting was an accident, the taxpayers would have saved a lot of money with the civil claim settlement. It was the cover-up, which the family lawyer correctly alleged, that made things far worse for the city financially. Bob Bennett just had to sit back and watch Freeman's prosecutors destroy the credibility of Noor and almost everyone else with MPD. And that was exactly what happened in the case of *State of Minnesota v. Mohamed Noor*.

Chapter Thirteen

The Appeal

It probably seems odd that the defense was appealing when the Franklin case had not yet gone to trial. But after the appeal document was filed in December of 2016, we would then receive a briefing schedule from the Eighth Circuit Court of Appeals. This was a significant matter. This appellate court could reverse Judge Frank's decision and order him to dismiss the case.

We were going on over two and a half years after we started the lawsuit and three and a half after Terrance had been killed. It seemed that delay was a strategy for our opponent.

Our opponent's appellate brief, called Appellants' Principal Brief, was filed with the Eighth Circuit on January 30, 2017. The brief was basically a verbatim regurgitation of what they argued with Judge Frank for summary judgment in 2016. It was 47 pages in length with three large booklets of exhibits. They requested 20 minutes of oral argument.

We filed our opposition brief, Appellee's Principal Brief, 31 pages in length, on March 1, 2017. Our arguments were essentially the same as our opposition to the defense summary judgment motion.

Although the Court was based out of St. Louis, Missouri, the panel judges would come to St. Paul periodically for oral argument for Minnesota cases. Our hearing took place on October 19, 2017. There are 13 circuit courts in the United States, consisting of 11 judges each. The judges are randomly assigned to each case. We drew Circuit Judge James Loken, Circuit Judge Clarence Beam, and Circuit Judge Steven Colloton. At the time the decision was rendered on December 26, 2017, Judge Loken was 77 years old, and Judge Beam was 87 years old. Judge Colloton seemed like a kid at only 54 years old, but the two elder judges looked much younger to me, and both were really intelligent and understood the case issues in detail. Judges on the U.S. Circuit Courts were typically brilliant, and they had an advantage over jurors – they could ask the lawyers questions. U.S. Supreme Court appointees usually evolved from the circuit courts. With the question reality, a lawyer could look really bad in the span of a second.

I had some experience with appellate practice in state court having argued a few cases with the Minnesota Court of Appeals and two with the Minnesota Supreme Court. This was the first time I had ever argued a case with the Eighth Circuit.

Brian Carter argued for the defense and did a good job, although I disagreed with every contention he made to support his clients' position for immunity and dismissal.

I began, and then one of the judges, Judge Beam, asked me if the Court even had jurisdiction over this appeal. I had not perceived this issue at all and had to capitulate to the Court that I did not know the answer.

Months later, on December 26, 2017, the Court issued its decision with an opinion written by Circuit Judge Beam. The "Judgment" read, in relevant part, "After consideration, it is hereby ordered and adjudged that the appeal is dismissed for lack of jurisdiction in accordance with the opinion of the Court."

From our team's perspective, we had prevailed and really did not care much about the detail, but things would not end there – far from it. However, the decision was interesting and was not unanimous. Circuit Judge Beam noted the facts concerning the time gap and the absence of blood on the MP5 as important to Judge Frank's decision to deny qualified immunity. The defense argued, strangely, that those facts were not material or blatantly contradicted by the record. Circuit Judge Beam held: "The problem with this argument, however, is that the district court did not hold that the facts relayed in its recitation were undisputed, and more importantly, we lack jurisdiction to review the factual issues that abound in this appeal." Circuit Judge Beam then cited United States Supreme Court precedent in the form of case law.

Circuit Judge Beam went on to conclude: "While we have jurisdiction to determine whether conduct the district court deemed sufficiently supported for purposes of summary judgment constitutes a violation of clearly established law, we lack jurisdiction to determine whether the evidence could support a finding that particular conduct occurred at all." Case law was again cited. In essence, the court was saying that the factual disputes were appropriate for a jury, not a substantive legal issue on appeal.

The scary reality was this: Circuit Judge Loken dissented. He actually felt that Peterson and Meath were entitled to qualified immunity, and the denial of same by Judge Frank was error. If one of the other two judges had agreed with him, our case would have probably been over. We breathed a big sigh of relief. Our concern was could jurors believe Peterson and Meath if this judge did?

But our opponents were not done. They then requested "en banc" review, a Latin term that means "in full." Litigants who lose on appeal with circuit courts typically request this. If granted, the entire circuit's judges hear the appeal, all 11, and then another decision is rendered. With a 2-1 decision, en banc review is more likely to be granted.

On February 16, 2018, with an order of that date, the Court denied the petition for rehearing en banc. Additionally, the Court denied a rehearing with the original panel.

Our opponents were hell bent on ensuring that the case never saw the light of day with a jury. Would they stop here or continue? On May 17, 2018, Brian Carter, on behalf of the defendants, filed a writ of certiorari requesting review with the Supreme Court of the United States. Review with the Supreme Court was discretionary. Only about 2.5% of all filed cases were accepted for review. Writs were usually quickly discarded.

But we had concern, and it was legitimate. On May 21, 2018, Carter was advised of the writ filing "placed on the docket" by Case Analyst, Redmond K. Barnes. Three days later, in a concise small booklet brief "Petitioners," previously the defendants and the appellants, filed "Petition for Writ of Certiorari" with the Supreme Court. It was in the name of Susan Segal, Sara Lathrop, and Brian Carter. Tim Skarda had apparently just retired.

Around this time frame, I provided a "Waiver" on behalf of "Respondent," Walt Franklin's title now, which opined that we would not be filing a response to the petition. We thought that would be the end of it. It was not. Approximately two months later, with a letter dated July 19, 2018, Clerk of the Court, Scott Harris, asked that I submit a "response" to the writ filed on May 17, 2018. This was in the category of unbelievable, and I promptly contacted co-counsel Jay Deratany and Mike Kosner to assist with the logistics of the response.

Was it possible the Supreme Court could accept review of an interlocutory appeal that the Eighth Circuit dismissed for lack of jurisdiction for what seemed like a well-reasoned decision by the majority and the rejection of an en banc request? We had legitimate concern, and this was why. In May of 2015, the Supreme Court sided with two San Francisco police officers who had shot a mentally ill woman who possessed a knife. The case was *San Francisco v. Sheehan*. The facts concerned police called to a group home by the woman's social worker. She objected to officers coming in, grabbed a knife, and threatened to kill them. She was shot and pepper sprayed. Justice Breyer recused himself because his brother, a federal judge at the district court level, dismissed the case in 2011. But the Ninth Circuit U.S. Court of Appeals had reversed Judge Breyer. Now, the Supreme Court was reversing the Ninth Circuit. In basically a unanimous decision, Justice Samuel Alito wrote the opinion that the officers had the right to enter the woman's room and the right to use force when she approached them with a knife.

It was hard to criticize this opinion. It was a bad test cast, I felt, but the precedent could be applied to our case although the Franklin case was clearly distinguishable. We of course had strong evidence Terrance was murdered, and we were obviously hopeful the writ would be rejected after we submitted our response. Jay and Mike's firm handled opposing the writ and did a good job pointing out why the Supreme Court should deny review.

But there was another concern. Things never seemed to be easy for this case. In April of 2018, the Supreme Court rendered a decision concerning a case from Arizona, another interlocutory appeal. In that case, *Kisela v. Hughes*, a Tucson woman was shot four times outside of her home because she was seen carrying a large knife. As reported by the *Los Angeles Times* on April 2, 2018: "The ruling – which comes at a time of growing controversy over police shootings nationwide – effectively advises courts to rely more heavily on the officer's view of such incidents, rather than the victim's." It was a 7-2 decision.

Justices Sonia Sotomayor and Ruth Bader Ginsburg voted in a strongly worded dissent that the person shot had not threatened anyone including the police. In response to the decision, many were livid including Justice Sotomayor who said, "[The] decision is not just wrong on the law; it also sends an alarming signal to law enforcement officers and the public. It tells officers they can shoot first and think later."

It was not just those on the left who criticized the decision. As noted in the *L.A. Times* article, Clark Neily, vice president of the libertarian Cato Institute, said: "Today's ruling gives yet another green light to officers who use deadly force as a tool of first resort instead of last." He went on: "It does so based on a legal doctrine – qualified immunity – that the Supreme Court invented out of whole cloth to help create a policy of near-zero accountability for law enforcement."

David Cole, of the American Civil Liberties Union, said, "Giving a free pass to officers under these circumstances will only exacerbate the problem."

The *Sheehan* and *Kisela* cases perhaps explained why our opponent was hell bent on getting Franklin up to the Supreme Court. But in some respects, those two cases could be a negative for them in the sense that if the Court had recently spoken on federal law regarding police shooting cases, they might be less inclined to review another one. We were reasonably confident that they would deny the petition even though we submitted a response. If review was accepted, that alone did not mean the Eighth Circuit would be reversed, but it would not be a good sign for this type of fact situation considering *Sheehan* and *Kisela*, but certainly, the Franklin case was much different.

On October 29, 2018, the Supreme Court of the United States denied the defendants' attempted appeal by denying the petition. Libor Jany reported the development in an October 30, 2018 *Strib* story. I was quoted that I was not surprised by the Court's decision but that "it took a long time, so it was a little disconcerting." I disguised my real worry coming off as a tough guy.

Reference was made to a settlement conference for Franklin in April of 2018. The defendants' offer was nothing.

In the story, I referenced a trial date in six to nine months. It would eventually be October of 2019 – in exactly a year. We had dodged another bullet, so to speak, on what had become a long journey due to no fault of our own. It was now 5½ years since Terrance had been killed, and 6 ½ years, best-case scenario, to finally get our day in court. This did not seem like justice.

But would our opponent reconsider going to trial and potentially resolve the case? Were the events that had been going on around us in Minnesota and elsewhere relevant to them? The disastrous trial and settlement of Damond – the worst in the agency's history - had yet to happen. It was six months away.

Chapter Fourteen
The Closing and Closure

The year 2018 trickled into 2019. We had confirmation of an October, 2019 trial date for the Franklin case. Finally, I would begin trial prep three months before in July, which was plenty of time. I gave our experts and others like Cala Scott and Ashley Martin a heads up on the date and that they would all have to testify. There was no indicator going into 2019 – or before – that the City of Minneapolis had any intention of settling or even making an anemic offer. The named defendants Harteau, Peterson, and Meath would never be required to pay anything out of pocket whether the case settled or if the defendants were on the hook for a jury verdict. The city was fully defending and indemnifying – paying – if any of the defendants were found to be civilly liable. It did not matter to us or to Walt who would be paying.

In February of 2019, a local Fox 9 reporter, Tom Lyden, disclosed publicly a video from the Ramsey County Jail in St. Paul of a young black male being physically abused by jail staff – deputies employed by the Ramsey County Sheriff's Office. The 13-minute video went viral, and it seemed like everyone in a political position of power in the Twin Cities, including the Ramsey County Sheriff, expressed outrage at the conduct.

The black male in question was 24-year-old Terrell Wilson, and he would hire me soon after the video went public. I had nothing to do with Lyden securing the video, and neither did Terrell. The video was from almost three years prior on April 13, 2016, and when Lyden visited Terrell, before I was hired, Terrell had no idea his assault had been depicted on video. This was not jail video. A deputy actually recorded it himself with a hand-held device ostensibly to document that the beating was reasonable in light of Terrell's conduct. There was one major problem with this plan: Terrell did not resist at all. Terrell . . . a young brother with dreads like Terrance Franklin.

163

The video revealed that after being repeatedly beaten and pepper sprayed, Terrell can be heard saying: "Please don't kill me. Please don't kill me. I'm sorry." Although Terrell had not spit, the officers put a spit guard on him, which affected his breathing. During the video, a deputy, Travis VanDeWiele, as reported by Lyden, forced Terrell to his knees as Terrell was seated and strapped into a jail-seat device. Terrell then said repeatedly, "I can't breathe. I can't breathe." He was crying and pleading with the officers to stop. VanDeWiele punched and kneed him many times in the chest area.

As Terrell slipped in and out consciousness, he said: "God won't let me die."

The fall out was immediate. The deputy who was most aggressive in the video, VanDeWiele, was forced to resign, which he did on February 24, but the public learned that he was on paid leave for two years before he resigned. If the video was not bad enough, that fact really outraged citizens.

Quotes came from all corners especially regarding the concept of positional asphyxiation, which almost killed Terrell. The assaultive conduct involved six correctional officers. The officers all issued reports that were complete contradictions with the video.

Lyden secured the opinions of various use-of-force experts who agreed, unanimously, that Terrell was never combative with the jailers or otherwise a threat. Lyden's Fox story of February 25, 2019 included a quote from Christine Cole, Executive Director of the Crime and Justice Institute, a think tank that studies excessive force cases. Cole said, "I thought it was one of the most distressing videos I've seen. This was really bad, I thought. This was just violence, power . . . and being pissed off."

A former LAPD Senior Detective Supervisor, Tim Williams, noted: "Mr. Wilson is trying to comply, but he can't when four or five different things are being done to him."

The sheriff at the time was Matt Bostrom, not the current sheriff, Bob Fletcher. Bostrom previously resigned to take a job in Maryland, and the Ramsey County Board appointed Jack Serier as sheriff. Serier tried to fire VanDeWiele but to no avail. VanDeWiele's leave began on February 8, 2017. Sheriff Fletcher was then elected in January of 2019, soon before the video became public.

Sheriff Fletcher stepped up to the plate, and said: "[The video] is extremely disturbing and demonstrated failed supervision and poor training." And then said: "The employees who witnessed it had a duty to intervene, to stop the assaultive tactics and the use of excessive force." It was refreshing to see a law enforcement leader speak the truth. Law enforcement personnel were standing by and not doing anything. How that concept would reverberate in May of 2020.

I moved quickly. By early June of 2019, I was able to secure a settlement for Terrell in the amount of $525,000 from Ramsey County. The settlement received large publicity in and outside of Minnesota. The publicity of this case, it seemed to our team, probably helped us with the Franklin case.

By December of 2019, correctional officers at the Ramsey County Jail started wearing body cams. It was reported that this was a direct result of the Terrell Wilson matter. It felt great to make a difference. For Terrell's part, he gave the credit to Tom Lyden and me as his attorney. Sheriff Fletcher deserved credit also. I gave the credit to my courageous client, Lyden, and a technology known as video. Sadly, the bottom line was that nobody would have believed any of this if it was described verbally but for the video. This included Terrell. He would have not been believed. Even as of 2019, this was a sad reality for young black males when law enforcement lined up against them. Video became the great equalizer.

When I began my Franklin trial prep in July of 2019, I decided to put together a closing argument and planned to tweak/change it from that point forward up to and even during the trial. In a civil trial, the "closing" or "summation" as it is commonly called in legal parlance, is incredibly important. It gives a lawyer the ability to tie all of the evidence together, and with the application of the law, as explained by the trial judge, the ability to suggest to the jury exactly how to fill out the verdict form – questions the jury must answer to decide the outcome of the case. Also, a lawyer can engage in argument in the closing – not permitted in the opening.

Although how I would deliver the closing to the jury in Franklin could change depending on the evidence at trial, I already knew essentially what it was from the massive case file and the great resource of the discovery depositions. What I am presenting here is only a portion of that part of the closing that dealt with liability, that is, did Terrance Franklin's death result from excessive, unreasonable force? This was presented to my co-counsel for review in a report from July of 2019 – a sample closing never disclosed publicly until in this book. The damages part was a separate argument presented in a separate report.

Proposed Closing re. Liability for Trial Team – by Mike P.

Ladies and gentlemen, you now know the law as Judge Frank has explained it to you. Although the actual law can be fairly complicated, it basically can be broken down in this fashion: Federal law prevents a police officer from engaging in excessive force when interacting with a citizen. It's really that simple. Here, we know from the evidence, we don't have to guess, that what Officers Peterson and Meath did to Terrance Franklin was murder, and therefore, excessive force and wrongful death.

The burden of proof in a civil case is preponderance of the evidence. What this means is that the plaintiff only has to tip the scale ever so slightly beyond 50% to meet his or her burden of proof on a particular issue. You probably have heard the description for burden of proof in a criminal case, which is beyond a reasonable doubt. Folks knowledgeable of the law agree unanimously that this burden description is a more difficult one to reach than preponderance of the evidence for a civil case. But even if Mr. Franklin was required to meet the higher criminal case standard or, in fact, beyond all doubt, which he is not required to do, hasn't he met his burden of proof that these two officers not only engaged in excessive force, but in fact murdered his son?

I think it's clear that all of the basement SWAT officers thought that there were no witnesses, which is understandable. There certainly weren't any citizens down in that basement. It was only them. But technology caught up with them. But if you think about it, there was a massive amount of additional evidence to support Mr. Gaines' video device, which proved all alone that this was a case of murder, and the so-called official MPD version of what supposedly happened was bogus, nothing but a legal gimmick, a complete farce.

Remember that it is you, and only you, who are the decision makers for the facts of this case. Those questions that need to be answered on the issue of liability are on the verdict form that will be presented to you. I will comment on that later. I am first going to address the issue of liability, that is, excessive force, and I will then move on to damages.

When we talk about liability, let's address the facts of the case. In looking at the facts, perhaps the best place to start is the evidence that was presented as to what first happened at the apartment complex on Lyndale, which was the beginning of this entire situation.

There were three members of law enforcement who were involved with the initial interaction, and their reports were certainly confusing especially when compared to the apartment surveillance video that visually depicted the entire event. There is no audio, but the witnesses filled in the blanks as to what was said. As you may recall, those three individuals were Sgt. Katherine Smulski, Sgt. Gerald Moore, and the Department of Corrections officer, Dave Schiebel.

The issues at this point were: What really happened in terms of Terrance's exit out of the parking lot? Did it appear that he was trying to run over and therefore injure or kill Sgt. Smulski? And also, and this is really important, what were these three members of law enforcement telling other police personnel in the field about what happened – in person and via police radio after that event ended?

Fortunately, a lot of this confusion is solved, like what occurred in the Bickal basement, with video. You folks saw the apartment parking lot video. It is clear from those images that Terrance was not attempting to run anyone over at all. He merely backed up slowly - as even Sgt. Smulski agreed was true - and he then drove away.

It is important to note that Terrance may not even have been arrested. They were probably just going to question him. And just because a witness thought he may have been responsible for a burglary a week or so before does not mean Terrance did anything wrong. It could have been a case of mistaken identity or some other explanation. But since he was killed, we will never know if he would have been charged, and if he was charged, whether the case would have been dismissed, or whether he would have been found not guilty by a judge or jury of his peers.

167

It seemed obvious that Terrance had no interest in speaking with law enforcement. Why is that? Hard to know. Importantly, though, he was behaving peaceably with Ms. Holman and her two children when the police came over to her apartment complex. Why young males flee can run the gamut. Maybe he had a small amount of marijuana on his person and got rid of it when he was in flight. That would be a petty misdemeanor, not even a crime as defined under Minnesota law. After the situation became enflamed, something he saw with his own eyes, he got scared, and we know that from Cala Scott and Bamnet Woldegabriel. That is why he was intent on not being found. That intention of not being found does not mean at all that he would have resisted when found. And the evidence from the Gaines' key video clip makes clear that he gave up. He capitulated regardless of what the five SWAT officers said, which I will get to later.

There is no question Terrance sinned. He should not have tried to get away, and he should not have broke into the Bickal home to hide. That second act arose out of self-preservation. I mean at the beginning, Dave Schiebel even came up to him with gun drawn. Terrance was probably worried they were going to beat him up and sic a tough police dog on him. And that is exactly what they did. He was a scared rabbit trying to avoid the inevitable – an assault by the police. He had sinned. In the grand scheme, they weren't big sins. But his conduct did not merit a death sentence especially since he gave up right away when they found him.

Let's talk about Sgt. Smulski. She comes into this courtroom, looks you folks in the eyes, under oath, and tells you that it was her belief that Terrance Franklin was trying to injure or kill her. But there are two big problems with that contention: The apartment video doesn't show that, and she says nothing about the notion Terrance tried to kill or injure her in her written report. Why is it not there? Because it didn't happen.

Think about this: If you are a police officer, and you believe someone has tried to run you over with a car, isn't that the main point you would want to make in your report after the incident? And wouldn't you also let others in the field who didn't witness it know about that right away? She says she never radioed that information to others, but she has no problem telling Cala Scott at the scene: "He tried to kill me." It's almost as if people like Smulski and Moore don't want to be responsible for a murder because in their mind, for MPD personnel like Peterson and Meath, they know that fact alone could cause officers with that mindset to commit murder.

So what is going on here? These witnesses want you to think that Terrance was trying to kill a police officer, but on the other hand, they want to make you think they didn't tell anyone about it. It's like that saying, they want to have their cake and eat it too.

So it is clear Smulski exaggerated to others in the field what happened to her, and that's what led in part to the feeding frenzy of officers running all over this neighborhood with their guns drawn. It's what Jimmy Gaines and Anthony Oberlander told you – they could tell from what they observed that something bad was going to happen. And that's what prompted Jimmy to record with his iPod Touch. Without that, it's entirely possible the truth never would have come out.

The feeding frenzy was additionally supported by Jim Bickal, Cala Scott, and Bamnet Woldegabriel. I won't repeat their testimony on this topic, but we know from them that many officers were running around the neighborhood with guns drawn. We now know why.

So then we have Sgt. Moore. He admits his report is not accurate about Sgt. Smulski jumping out of the way. But he says this only after seeing the video. So his report was an exaggeration.

But then he says he never told anyone that day that the suspect Terrance had attempted to run over Sgt. Smulski. The problem with that is Officers Muro and Staufenberg both admitted that while they were in the SWAT van headed to the scene they heard over the radio that the suspect had rammed a vehicle and tried to run over an officer. So who was this? We know from Officer Durand it was Sgt. Moore who said this. Remember Officer Durand testifying to that? It was the voice of Sgt. Moore, and it was said, according to Durand, that the suspect nearly struck a 5th Precinct supervisor. The feeding frenzy was on.

So if these three SWAT members knew, Peterson, Meath, and Stender also had to know. Ladies and gentlemen, even though it was not true, in the moments before those five SWAT officers went into Jim Bickal's basement, they thought the man who they knew was down there, Terrance Franklin, had tried to kill a fellow officer. It's obvious how that is relevant to what happened on May 10, 2013.

And "rammed a vehicle"? This ended up being a small amount of paint transfer not requiring body work. Another exaggeration. You saw that evidence.

One more point I'd like to make about this initial situation at the apartment complex on Lyndale. Dave Schiebel, DOC Dave they call him, says he thought Terrance was trying to kill Sgt. Smulski, but like her, he doesn't note that in his report. And then does not radio anyone about this because he felt that was the obligation of Smulski and Moore. Credibility, ladies and gentlemen. Credibility. If Dave Schiebel is not honest about this, can you believe anything else he says in terms of critical details? And why did he walk up to the P.T. Cruiser with gun drawn? Terrance had to have seen this. I will talk further about Schiebel later.

So what happened in that basement? If you think about it, the Gaines' audio really provides a road map. You have heard that audio repeatedly during this trial. I hope it was not too much. But I ask you to please listen to it closely when you deliberate.

At second 11 of the main video clip, you hear MTC Officer Geoffrey Wyatt, say, "Officer shot!" Now we know from his testimony that time had elapsed after he knew an officer had been shot up to the time he said that.

He told you it took 5 to 10 seconds to get from the front of the house to the side. The north door was open. This was after he heard via his shoulder radio that an officer had been shot. He then was at that spot, he estimated, for 20 seconds. He then headed back to get his first aid kit – which was another 5 to 10 seconds.

That adds up to, giving the defendants the benefit of the doubt, about 30 seconds. So therefore, from the time an officer had been shot 19 seconds elapsed, and then Jimmy began to record for that clip. Recall, Gaines' video was not on when the two officers were shot. At second 11, Wyatt then says "officer shot," which pretty much everyone in the case admits to hearing. But here's the thing: At second nine, you can hear, "My name is Mookie." This is 28 seconds after an officer had been shot. But that's huge on many levels. That was the nickname Terrance self-applied, and if he was saying his name, ladies and gentlemen, doesn't that prove that he had been successfully

170

apprehended? It would be the first question the police would ask: What's your name? And all five basement SWAT officers said Terrance never spoke a word. Doesn't that fact alone cause you to question the truth and veracity of every one of these officers and therefore everything they allege about what happened in that basement?

Peterson and Meath murdered Terrance, and the other three, Stender, Muro, and Durand helped them get away with it.

This can then be heard at second 26: "Damn freakin nigger." The cops are angry. This is 45 seconds after two officers have been shot. Then, at second 27: "Man, let me go." Again, you heard numerous witnesses testify that this is Terrance. Is that understandable? Sure. He was mad because they are calling him a racist name.

It all ties together. It all makes sense.

So then we have at second 43, 62 seconds after the officers were shot: "Come out little nigger! Don't go putting those hands up now!" So you may be asking: Why would Terrance be given those voice directives if he had already been apprehended at least by second 9, or 28 seconds after an officer had been shot? I submit this is what happened: The SWAT team was dealing with the two officers who had been shot, and left Terrance for a few moments. Terrance probably hunkered down away from things – like in a corner. It seems clear he would have fear that they would seek retribution against him because two cops had been accidentally shot. And isn't that exactly what happened?

An officer tells him to "come out" meaning come towards him. I would submit that was Peterson. Terrance complies, and to confirm his capitulation, he puts his hands up in the air. And that really gets Peterson mad. "Don't go putting those hands up now" is the law enforcement way of saying: "Why didn't you give up sooner?"

Doesn't this all make sense?

So then they grab him by the dreads – at least Peterson does – which he admitted to in this courtroom. Dreads were found on the basement floor after. Terrance is dragged into the little laundry room. Peterson and his long-time friend Meath kill Terrance together. You can hear those volleys at second 53. Those are clearly gunshots – a series of them – as expert Mr. Drago, a long-time member of law enforcement told you. Those are the volleys that killed Terrance

171

Franklin. This is 72 seconds after the officers were accidentally shot – an eternity under these facts. If Terrance Franklin grabbed that MP5 and shot two officers, he would have been dispatched immediately. We know that. Every cop down there had a sidearm. Peterson said "seconds" from MP5 discharge to the killing of Terrance. He lied to you.

And there is something else. Isn't it an interesting fact that the door for that little laundry room was closed? Why . . . you might ask? It was closed – probably by Peterson – so the others wouldn't see the dirty deed they were about to commit. How do we know the door was closed? Peterson said so. Stender said so. And Muro noted at various times during the fracas that the door was closed. Peterson and Meath did not want the others to see what they were about to do. Terrance Franklin never should have ended up in that room. Nash found him by the water heater – in a separate room. There is no rational explanation as to how Terrance ended up in that little room. Recall that Durand was asked that question. His answer? "I don't know." That answer alone should tell you a lot about this case.

The door was closed . . . that's not a little fact, folks. It's a big one and when combined with other evidence makes clear Terrance was in fact murdered.

This was a brutal execution-type killing. You heard from Dr. Boeding who performed the autopsy. Multiple rounds entered the right side of Terrance's head – including, for example, into the right ear and right temple. Mr. Ernest told you about the downward angle of declination. We know from people like Meath that Terrance was on the ground when he was killed.

Let's move onto the DNA. Terrance's DNA was on the gun. We know why – the explanation is such that it was innocently on the gun. DOC Dave Schiebel solved that riddle. I'm sure you folks recall, but let me remind you quickly. Schiebel puts his hands on Terrance's body to check for signs of life. He is then handed the MP5 by Durand. He tells you he has gloves on, but he no longer has the gloves, and nobody can vouch for him that he was in fact wearing gloves. And he mentions nothing about the gloves in his report.

Folks, this was a bald faced lie. How do we know? His DNA is all over the MP5, something Chief Harteau failed to tell the public in September of 2013.

This investigation was a whitewash. True and simple. A cover-up. Blame Terrance Franklin for the embarrassing reality of an accidental discharge that injured two officers – and the embarrassment of the motorcycle crash over 30 minutes after Terrance was killed that you heard about during the trial.

This investigation, which was a joke, never should have been handled in-house. This case reveals what happens when an investigation is not conducted objectively.

Sgts. Porras and Kjos either failed to uncover the truth or just ignored it hopeful nobody would figure it out. It's really embarrassing if you think about it.

To say they blew it is a bold statement. I don't like people who make assertions without facts. But there are facts here. Many of them. Let's first talk about the time-gap problem. Officer Sporny – who clearly issued a report that was truthful to the best of his ability – made clear from his description that after sounds such that they indicated the time the two officers were shot – there was then a 20-30 second gap – when he then heard 8-10 volleys. It's obvious those were the gunshots of Peterson and Meath killing Terrance.

It seems clear that Sporny's estimate was not accurate since a better source is the Gaines' video clip that has the gap over 60 seconds when combined with Officer Wyatt's testimony. Recall, Mr. Harrington was able to match the video metadata to the actual police radio comms – within one second. But the point is any competent investigator would have viewed the Sporny report as a big red flag that perhaps the basement SWAT team was not telling the truth about what went down in that basement.

They did nothing. They completely ignored the time-gap problem.

How about the Gaines' video clip? They completely ignored that too. They claim they did not have the ability to enhance in house. Okay. Why not hire an expert like we did with Ed Primeau?

That evidence cried out to be analyzed! Why didn't they? Because they knew it would break down their final conclusion of a clean kill. Clean kill? It was anything but.

You heard from Mr. Primeau. He gave you a perfectly valid, scientific explanation as to how voices and words from that basement

173

could have been picked up by Mr. Gaines' device. I won't repeat that. I'm sure you remember it.

Ladies and gentlemen I thank you for your patience. I just have a few more areas I'd like to touch on covering this issue of liability. And those are Mark Durand, the MP5, and whether Terrance was responsible for the shooting of the two officers. I will close with why Terrance Franklin was murdered.

Let me first address the interesting fact that the MP5 after this event was over had no blood on it. Not even a speck of blood. You heard the various witnesses including Lucas Peterson that there was blood everywhere in that little laundry room. The MP5 could not have been in that room when Terrance was killed. And if it was not in that room, Durand could not have been in that room. Recall that the gun was with Durand the whole time connected to his body with a harness.

Durand is not a murderer. His sin is participating with the cover-up. Think about this please. If he accidentally fired his gun injuring two of his fellow officers, he had two choices: Admit the truth whereupon he is outcast forever, or blame the young black male who one officer referred to at the scene as the "bad guy." Which is the easier path of least resistance for Durand and his career? Remember, FS Kristin Jacobson is an employee of MPD. What reason would she have to lie about there being no blood on the gun? She didn't lie. She told the truth. Like FS Brenda Hummel. She told the truth also.

But here's the problem for Durand – what does the evidence show about who is responsible for the discharge of the rounds from his gun? Stender, Muro, and Meath have literally no clue as to why or how or who was responsible for the gun going off. Neither does Peterson, but remember what he says? The ridiculous testimony that Terrance pointed the MP5 at him and apparently decided not to shoot. Can anyone ever believe anything Peterson says after the Nancy Johnson incident? Recall that? A black woman was criminally charged because of his lie.

If Franklin had shot two officers, why spare Peterson? Seriously, how can anyone believe Lucas Peterson? It's interesting that it was a city-owned surveillance camera that caught Peterson in the Johnson lie.

174

But the best evidence Durand shot those two rounds – not Terrance Franklin – comes out of Durand's own mouth. It's what he said after the incident was over long before he ever had a chance to talk to a union lawyer. Recall that? He tells Sgt. Strauss: "It was my gun, Sarge." That was almost an apology. This is the type of thing an officer would say if he's trying to lessen the blame for his mistake. In other words, why not blame the gun?

Then he tells DOC Dave – after handing him the MP5: "This is the gun that caused the injuries." Even Schiebel admitted that he had no idea what that meant, and it confused him. Again, this is something an officer would say to assuage or lessen his blame for a horrible mistake.

If Terrance really had accessed the gun, Durand would have said something like: "That's the gun the suspect grabbed and shot two of our guys. Can you believe that?" Or maybe a cuss word like call the suspect an "ass" or maybe even something harsher. In the grand scheme, ladies and gentlemen, these two comments, standing all alone, make clear it was Durand who was the one who shot that gun, accidentally, not Terrance Franklin. On the issue of liability, case closed…

And we know, we don't have to guess; we know that if Terrance Franklin shot that gun, he would have been killed immediately. The gap was at least 72 seconds – plenty of time for Peterson and Meath to do their dirty deed.

Folks, I don't want you to believe what I am saying is true just because I am one of the lawyers for the Franklin family. I want you to believe these things are true because the believable evidence dictates them to be true. The evidence is clear. It is concise. It is simple. It is right. It is just. And these five SWAT officers who concocted a story got caught. Pure and simple.

Lastly, you may be asking, why did this happen? What was their motivation? I am confident you folks have ideas in that regard. But let me make some suggestions as to why this happened. The facts make clear this was murder. That has been proven. But the reason, their motivation, would be considered corroborative circumstantial evidence to support the contention of murder.

There clearly was intense anger from the beginning. After the initial scenario at the apartment complex, it was clear every cop in the

175

field thought the suspect Franklin tried to kill an officer. We now know that wasn't true, but that was the message that was clearly disseminated long before the SWAT team went down those basement steps.

Do you really believe Lucas Peterson when he says that information did not amp him up? There's also an attempt by some to make it sound like the demeanor in the SWAT van going to the scene was happy-go-lucky. This is another example of the dishonesty in this case. The notion Franklin allegedly tried to run over a cop on Lyndale was motive enough for murder.

But there was a second big event that tied into why Peterson and Meath murdered Terrance: the accidental discharge. It is probable that nobody knew Meath was shot, including Meath, until a few minutes later – after Terrance was killed. Recall, the big message was "Officer shot" not "Officers shot." But certainly, everyone knew right away when Muro was shot.

This killing was not premeditated, but some time did go by. The key quote for motive was from the Gaines' clip: "Don't go puttin' those hands up now." And then earlier at second 27: "Damn freakin' nigger!" This probably was the voice of Peterson, but we don't know for sure. The murder was a knee-jerk reaction, just like the decision of Jimmy Gaines to activate his iPod Touch. And it is important to note that Peterson and Meath were long-time friends before they ever began working together with MPD. It was a combo-platter of these two things that led to murder, and the decision of both to be judge, jury, and executioner.

Who would dispute their description after Durand supported the absurd story? And then it was easy to get Stender and Muro to say some nonsense like Terrance said nothing during the entire event, didn't react to pain, and comments like: "He's got a gun!"

What you saw here, ladies and gentlemen, was The Blue Code of Silence - which is not just silence alone. It can include concocting a story to protect your guys. We stick together. We are not going to let this black male who didn't want to be caught destroy our careers. The truth has to be avoided, or Peterson and Meath end up charged with murder, and the other three are outcast from law enforcement forever. This is an illustration of how The Blue Code works.

176

That would conclude my closing argument on liability. I would however have gone over the verdict form on the specific questions, how the jury should answer each. Since no form had yet to be created, I will not speculate on what Judge Frank would have submitted with the input of the attorneys. I would have then moved on to damages, and I would have suggested specific compensation to be awarded as a result of these horrible facts, which led to the unjust death of a young man who did not deserve to die.

With the October of 2019 trial date fast approaching, there was a strange development in July. Judge Frank's staff inquired as to how many days each side would need for their presentation of the case. After consulting with Mike and Jay (it was decided Mike would second chair the case with me, that is, handle presentation of the case to the jury with me), we felt that after jury selection and opening statement we would need eight full days. Our opponent suggested they would need the same amount of time. This shocked us.

Our plan was to call almost every significant witness in the case in our case in chief, meaning our presentation, that is, the plaintiff's case. What this means is that all five of the SWAT team, DOC Dave, Sergeant Smulski, Sergeant Moore, and peripheral witnesses like Officer Sporny and others like Sergeant Kjos would all be called in our case. They would be questioned in cross-examination mode. This is what prosecutors did in *Noor*.

Normally when this occurs, the opposition proceeds with all of their questioning for each witness so that they do not need to call the same witness later in the case with their presentation. With their revelation of eight days, it appeared that their plan was to forego the questioning of each witness and then go ahead and call them later, but they were vague as to whether that would be the case.

When Judge Frank was apprised of this, he concluded that the time frame his office had committed to the case in October was not enough time to fit it in, and after addressing scheduling issues, it was agreed the trial date would be pushed out to April of 2020. As such, this case would finally be tried one month short of the seven-year anniversary of the incident that resulted in Terrance's death.

From our perspective, we had waited this long so we did not view it as a big deal. Neither did Walt. Still, it was difficult to believe that another significant chunk of time would go by before we would finally get our day in court. At this point, we still did not have any feedback from the opposition that they had any interest in settlement. My plan was to recommence with trial prep after the first of the year.

Another year had gone by. We were now into 2020. Mike Kosner contacted me and suggested that we reach out to the other side one last time to see if there would be interest with settling the case. I did not think this was possible since whenever the issue came up during the history of the case, which was not often, we were always told there would be no offer. Now that the dust had settled from all of their legal machinations, the strong evidence that we had developed was not a gray area. It was not going away. It was difficult for us to understand as to how our opponent was not able to perceive that this was not only a case of excessive force and wrongful death, but one of murder. Having said that, we had to accept the reality that what a jury could do was unpredictable. This time frame was just a few months before the Floyd tragedy, which would change everyone's perception of MPD. However, the Damond case was certainly a huge embarrassment, which folks in Minnesota had not forgotten.

Mike contacted Sara Lathrop. Amazingly, it sounded like the defendants were now interested in talking. Around the same time this dialogue began, we received an order from Magistrate Judge David Schultz, which ordered a settlement conference for February 11, 2020. Each civil case assigned in federal court in Minneapolis involves the assignment of a federal judge and a federal magistrate judge. The initial magistrate judge for our case had retired, and Magistrate Judge Schultz had not been on the case from the beginning but was very knowledgeable of the case facts. I liked him a lot and felt he was someone who could assist the parties with "mediating" a resolution. In complicated civil litigation, someone like this judge is imperative to get the parties to understand the pros and cons of their case, and Magistrate Judge Schultz fit this category well.

In 2013 when I first met Jay and Mike, I could see right away that Mike was not just a smart lawyer, but a litigator, someone who would be a lion in the courtroom. My impression was confirmed the more I got to know him that Mike was the perfect lawyer to be in a foxhole with. It also made sense for Mike to dialogue with Sara. Over the years, to a certain extent, I felt that bad blood had developed and even though I respected Sara and Brian Carter, I felt some anger for what I felt was a complete lack of understanding of how significant the evidence was. Of course, lawyers are great at bluffing and maybe that was not the case. In other words, maybe they realized they had major league problems with the evidence but were not letting our team know this. This is normal in civil litigation.

Rather than substantively negotiate, we felt it would be best to go through the settlement conference process with Judge Schultz and see if we could get it done.

Mike Kosner flew into town on February 10, 2020, and we had a meeting with Walt and Steve Rogers that evening. We had previously developed a strategy and submitted a position paper to Judge Schultz with a demand. It was unclear to us who would be making the decision for the city on settlement. But although we knew the City Council would have the final say in terms of approval, not the mayor, we reasonably assumed that Council President Lisa Bender would attend the mediation and be the point person for defense counsel on settlement. However, we really were not sure.

We appeared at the federal courthouse in Minneapolis on the morning of February 11. As trustee for the heirs, Walt Franklin had full settlement authority. Understandably, the years of waiting had really worn him out, and he was more inclined for closure rather than rolling the dice with the ambiguity as to what a jury could do. Although we certainly felt good about our evidence, we had to accept the fact that Terrance was in flight and as such, he was technically killed while committing a crime. We also had to remember that one of the three appellate judges with the Eighth Circuit actually believed the SWAT cops as to what happened in the basement. Having said that, an important gauge for me was Mike, and for weeks, he had gotten up to speed closely reading the file. He was on the same page with me for the notion that this was a murder, and although he was perfectly willing to go to trial, as was I, we both had to accept the potential risks.

The settlement conference itself was conducted in this fashion: The attorneys and their clients each went into separate rooms and would not actually come together until the end if there was resolution. Judge Schultz would then go back and forth conveying the demands and offers until hopefully the parties reached a settlement. As expected, he was a true professional and without his assistance, settlement may not have happened.

The process went on for many hours only broken up in the middle of the day for a half-hour lunch. I had handled hundreds of mediations, especially in my past as an insurance defense attorney, and I was very familiar with the process. In the summer of 2019, it took a skilled former federal judge, Judge James Rosenbaum, to assist with the mediation process for Terrell Wilson to successfully resolve that case. Judge Schultz had similar skills as Judge Rosenbaum.

Late in the afternoon we reached an agreement for settlement. Considering what had gone on previously, this was kind of a miracle. In cases involving municipalities, it is not possible to settle confidentially. As such, the settlement and the terms were disclosed publicly, and every major media outlet in the Twin Cities' market covered it. A reporter for each of the television stations came to my office the next few days for interviews.

We all came together in the courtroom, and sure enough, Lisa Bender was present along with Sara, Brian, and other representatives I do not recall. However, surprisingly, Chief Arradondo was also present. When we came in, Walt became emotional and was crying. The whole process from beginning to end had finally gotten to him. In a tremendous gesture of compassion and humanity, Chief Arradondo consoled him. This meant a lot to me on a personal level, and I will never forget it. Lisa Bender also showed a great deal of class.

The case settled for a sum of $795,000. In reaction to this, people fell in to one of three categories: 1. That was a great result; 2. That is about what I would have expected; and 3. It should have been a whole lot more. It is hard for me to comment on this. Ultimately what mattered to both Mike and me was that the client was happy. Could we have done better at trial? Possibly, but something like that is never a certainty. I had to admit though that the almost seven years had also worn me out, and the idea of closure was certainly attractive.

The people who were most shocked at the result were media and fellow attorneys. This is a common message I would hear: "Mike, how were you able to get them to pay anything? I never thought that any recovery was possible, and the case would be kicked out due to immunity." I appreciated comments like this, but the litigator in me at times wishes we would have rolled the dice with a jury. But even if we prevailed, another appeal would have been inevitable, and something like another three years of litigation was a possibility even with a successful jury verdict.

It was just a formality, but the City Council as a whole approved the settlement on February 14, 2020. For a case that for a long time did not receive media interest, it was surprising to me to see numerous television cameras outside of the room where the Council approved. Every television station covered the settlement. I was neutral in my comments. Not so for union president Bob Kroll. He ripped the city for the settlement and said in so many words that it was a sign of weakness. He actually called it a "slap in the face of justice." I was curious as to whether he read any legal pleadings in the case, but to us as a team and Walt too, we could have cared less how he felt.

What remained was a hearing later at the end of the month before Judge Frank. It was nice to see and talk off the record with Judge Frank. He was certainly happy the case resolved – at least that was my impression. Presiding over a four-week trial can be cumbersome.

The purpose of the hearing was to submit information to the judge to assist with the process of distributing the settlement funds to the various heirs.

The heirs were not required to attend, but Ashley Martin attended with her son, the son of both Ashley and Terrance, and Walt attended.

I did not know the family dynamics, but Walt had not seen his grandson in a while. It was a poignant scene. The boy was now 11 years old and seemed like a good kid. I thought to myself, will he research this case when he gets older to find out why he no longer has a father? I told Ashley I would always be there for him if he wants to talk. Judge Frank had a decision on distribution to us in a couple of weeks.

Rather than mailing a check, I brought it to Walt at his workplace in St. Paul. He was assembling high-end office furniture at various business locations.

I said, "Walt, well I guess this is it. I can't believe it's finally over. I was feeling it would never end."

"You did a good job, Mike. It was never an easy case. I now know that." he responded.

"It was a labor of love. I wonder if all of this will make a difference. What do you think?"

"I don't know," Walt said. "I have a feeling illegal killings will continue. What gets me really angry is the cover-up."

"I know. And they aren't easy to figure out. It involves a lot of hard work. Look at what went on in this case."

"It's crazy. I wonder if Minnesota will ever be in the news again like the shooting of that lady from Australia." Walt was prophetic.

When I had this conversation with Walt, it was just short of two months before all hell would break loose with the death of George Floyd on May 25, 2020.

I said goodbye to Walt and promised to stay in touch. I told him what a pleasure it was to represent him. He did not seem angry any more about all of it. He seemed to accept that what happened to his son was just how it was, almost a sad reality for African Americans in Minneapolis.

The Franklin case in some ways had taken energy out of me that I felt I would never get back. The whole thing seemed too crazy to be real. But it did actually happen. And I felt – thanks to the hard work and courage of a lot of good people, including citizens like Jimmy Gaines – that we were able to find out the truth, which sadly, in many endeavors in life is a goal that is never achieved.

I wondered over the course of history how many killings by the police never resulted in the true story coming out. Technology was changing that, as the pages of this book revealed, but what about the past? Unfortunately, there were many past mysteries that would never be solved. Thankfully the case of *Franklin v. City of Minneapolis*, et al., Court File No. 14-1467 (DWF/DTS) was no longer in that category.

Epilogue

I remember when I was a kid, maybe 11 years old. I lived with my family in a suburb of Washington, D.C. known as Adelphi, Maryland. When I was in elementary school, I had experienced bussing, and it did not affect me at all. I got along with white kids the same as with black kids. I think this was because of how I was raised.

I recall a black family in our neighborhood, one of only a few. I had befriended a couple of boys in the family who were around my age. One day, the local trash company refused to take the trash for this family. I had no idea why, but that did not sit well with my father, an ex-Marine, who had more influence on me than any man in my life. My father gave the trash company basically two choices: Take the trash, or get punched in the nose. Before it was over, the company took the trash, and the family never had any problems with trash removal from that point forward.

My father never said one word to me about it up until the day he passed away in January of 2015. He was a man who taught by example. Although he knew about the Franklin case, we had yet to begin the incredibly important discovery depositions. He was too sick for me to have any type of competent conversation with him about the case. I have often asked myself: Would my father be proud of how I handled the case? Would he agree with me that Terrance's death was a case of murder?

I do not believe anyone is born a racist. Racism is a learned trait. Would Terrance Franklin have been killed if he was white? How can I say, but it seemed clear to me that his race was relevant to how he died – and perhaps relevant as to how a police agency tried to help two really bad cops get away with it.

What makes someone like Lucas Peterson tick? What was his actual background to lead him to act the way he did in uniform? My team and I would never know, and even if he spoke on that topic, how would one know if it was the truth? Was it a bad experience or experiences in his early life that led him down this path? He was a smart man, but he chose the wrong path too often.

183

Within the four corners of this book, I believe, my team and I proved that Terrance Franklin was murdered. Would a Minnesota jury in federal court have reached the same conclusion? We felt that way, but we will never know for certain since Walt Franklin settled taking away the need for a trial, something we supported as a team.

My sincere hope is that those who have read this book found it interesting and hopefully educational even if they do not agree this was a case of murder. I completely respect that if that is their conclusion – as long as that belief is not born out of racism.

But for someone like me who has had black friends my whole life, there is no question in my mind that in some, if not all, segments of our society that young black males face hurdles that young men of other races do not face. Terrance Franklin found out the hard way. As soon as he left that apartment parking lot and grazed that squad car door, whether intentional or inadvertent, considering the history of the police agency he was tangling with, he was as good as dead.

In December of 2019, I was asked to attend the bail hearing for Curtis Flowers in Winona, Mississippi. This was a black man who went to trial six times for quadruple murder, and he was convicted every time. But each time, his conviction was reversed. Due to the amazing work of a St. Paul media company, APM Reports, a tremendous amount of evidence came to light, which made clear that this man was absolutely railroaded and was in fact truly innocent. There was no longer any credible evidence to support a conviction let alone any criminal charges.

The bail hearing went well. Curtis was released from prison that very day with strict parameters. But he could be recharged by a prosecutor named Doug Evans. It was believed by all in the know, however, that the case would just eventually go away. In September 2020, the Mississippi Attorney General dropped the charges against Flowers.

When I walked out of the courtroom, I looked up at the Mississippi flag. Embossed on a corner of that flag was the Confederate symbol. I do not have an axe to grind with the Confederacy or the South. The American Civil War was an incredibly important and historical event, and it is important to remember that the descendants of Confederate soldiers have been heroes in all of our

184

wars since. But seeing the Confederate flag within the borders of that state's flag, in my mind, helped to explain what happened to Flowers.

I took a picture of the flag at that time and sent it to some friends including Cory Hepola of WCCO Radio. Imagine Cory's response if I would have said to him: "This flag will change in June of 2020 because of something that happens in May of 2020 in Minnesota." He would have said I was crazy.

But sure enough, on June 30, 2020, the Mississippi legislature, with that state's governor, signed into law a bill removing the Confederate emblem. There was no dispute that a significant predicate to this historic event was the killing of a black man by a Minneapolis police officer in May of 2020. This was one example of many as to how George Floyd's death was changing the world.

Other miracles were happening because of George Floyd. In July of 2020, the Minnesota legislature, the only one in the entire nation with their house and senate controlled by different parties, worked out a "sweeping package of police accountability measures" as reported by the *Star Tribune*.

The bill, arguably the most significant in Minnesota history regarding law enforcement, included statewide bans on chokeholds and neck restraints, prohibitions of warrior-style training for officers, enhanced data collection for deadly force injuries, required officers to intervene (which did not happen in the Floyd matter), and created a new unit to investigate deadly force cases. Another interesting feature was the creation of a panel of arbitrators to handle police misconduct cases.

All of this was because a 17-year-old African American teenager, a smart young lady and citizen of Minneapolis, saw something that distressed her, grabbed her phone, and started recording on May 25, 2020. In addition to being about The Blue Code of Silence, one could say that maybe this book is about how the technology of video has changed the world. Terrance Franklin was a great example, but perhaps George Floyd has become the ultimate template.

At the time George Floyd was killed, I had tangled with MPD and their attorneys for what seemed like forever. I still have not processed, and perhaps never will fully process, the effect that tragic death has had on our nation and also worldwide.

This book describes an injustice that began with an unlawful killing and went through to the exoneration of the police officers by their own agency. It took the civil discovery process to uncover the truth and achieve some form of justice. One can only hope that the lessons learned from the Franklin case will prevent another of its type from ever happening again.

<u>Acknowledgments</u>

I want to acknowledge all who helped make this book possible. Walt Franklin was with me the whole journey and strongly endorsed my decision to write this book. He often said, "Mike, this story needs to be told, and you need to make sure everyone reads it." Nothing like pressure for an author.

Many thanks to my assistant, Michele Scherer, and law student Hayley Howe for their assistance with generating the manuscript. Without them, that task alone for me would have been next to impossible. It is not just a matter of typing. For example, generating the Cast of Character documents involved many logistics.

Those who assisted with content were Colleen Bray, Dave Bryan, and Robert Dudley. Their input was immeasurable, and without it I never could have generated the quality I think was achieved with this book. Robert has written three books of his own, and his input with the numerous questions I had throughout the project was incredibly helpful, especially since his books were of the same genre as mine.

The evolution and completion of the cover included Gregg Boury, and my brother Tim early on, then Cory and Terry Hepola, and finally, Mark Ziemba and Drea Solan. I recall when I first saw the cover, I was worried the content of the book would never match Drea's amazing graphic artist skills. We will leave it to the reader as to whether I came close.

A big thank you to the other manuscript readers: Alan Rogers, Karin Kidd, and Aimee Padden. My mother, Nancy Padden, provided me with great support with this project, as with all other endeavors in my life. And my in-laws, Gary and Loni Baumgartner, gave me excellent feedback for content.

Lastly, to my wife, Jill, and my son, Connor, for their patience with the great amount of time involved with this project.

News Stories

	Title	Date	Reporter	News Outlet	Chapter/page in book
1.	Officers Shot with Own Gun During South Mpls Fight in Satisfactory Condition	May 11, 2013	Cassie Hart	KSTP, Channel 5 (ABC)	Ch. 1, page 7
2.	Crash 35 Minutes After Cops Shot	May 12, 2013	Joy Powell	Star Tribune	Ch. 1, page 9
3.	Two Cops Wounded, Suspect Dies in South Minneapolis Shootout	May 11, 2013	Tad Vezner	Pioneer Press	Ch. 1, page 8
4.	Uptown Mayhem: 2 Dead, 2 Officers Shot	May 11, 2013	Joy Powell; Matt McKinney	Star Tribune	Ch. 1, page 9
5.	Man Killed in Struggle With Mpls. Police Was Shot Multiple Times	May 12, 2013	Dave Chanen	Star Tribune	Ch. 1, page 9
6.	Two Officers Recovering After Fridays	May 12, 2013	No Byline	Pioneer Press	Ch. 1, page 9

	Shooting				
7.	Family of Man Killed by Minneapolis Police Want Answers	May 13, 2013	Elizabeth Dunbar; Brandt Williams	MPR News	Ch. 1, page 9
8.	Terrance Franklin Shot Multiple Times by MPD, but it's Unclear whether He Fired a Shot Himself	May 13, 2013	Aaron Rupar	City Pages	Ch. 1, page 10
9.	Questions Swirl After Shots, Fatal Crash	May 13, 2013	Dave Chanen	Star Tribune	Ch. 1, page 10
10.	Suspect Fired an Officer's Gun	May 18, 2013	Dave Chanen; Matt McKinney	Star Tribune	Ch. 1, page 11
11.	Tasered During Traffic Stop, Minneapolis Man Asks Why	March 8, 2010	Matt McKinney	Star Tribune	Ch. 2, page 17
12.	Mpls. Police Officials Investigate Traffic Arrest	March 3, 2010	Caroline Lowe	WCCO, Channel 4 (CBS)	Ch. 2, page 17
13.	Few Cops	June 2,	Alejandra	Star	Ch. 2, page 18

	Censured Over Costly Decisions	2013	Matos; Randy Furst	Tribune	
14.	Police Shooting to be Reviewed	June 8, 2013	Matt McKinney	Star Tribune	Ch. 2, page 19
15.	13 Excessive Force Complaints Against Minneapolis Cop Involved in Shooting; One Cop, 13 Cases, $700K in Payouts	June 30, 2013	Alejandra Matos; Matt McKinney	Star Tribune	Ch. 2, page 19
16.	2 Cops Accused of Using Slurs	July 27, 2013	Dave Chanen; Matt McKinney	Star Tribune	Ch. 3, page 23
17.	2 MPD Cops Suspended; Racial, Sexual Slurs Alleged	July 27, 2013	Mark Albert	KSTP, Channel 5 (ABC)	Ch. 3, page 24
18.	Cops' Use of Slurs, Insults Detailed in Report, Video; Mpls. Cops Reportedly Used Slurs in Green Bay	July 30, 2013	Matt McKinney	Star Tribune	Ch. 3, page 25
19.	Cops'	July 31,	Matt	Star	Ch. 3, page 26

	"Hateful" Slurs Appall City Leaders	2013	McKinney	Tribune	
20.	Franklin Supporters See Parallels to Trayvon Martin Case	August 1, 2013	Abby Simons	Star Tribune	Ch. 4, page 27
21.	3 More Mpls. Cops Had Racial Altercation	August 2, 2013	Matt McKinney	Star Tribune	Ch. 4, page 27
22.	Mpls. Cops Accused of Racial Bias for Years	August 4, 2013	Matt McKinney; Randy Furst	Star Tribune	Ch. 4, page 27
23.	Terrance Franklin's DNA Found on Trigger	August 15, 2013	Dave Chanen	Star Tribune	Ch. 4, page 28
24.	No Mpls. Cops Disciplined After 439 Complaint Cases	August 28, 2013	Randy Furst	Star Tribune	Ch. 4, page 29
25.	Grand Jury Clears Officers in Suspects Shooting Death	September 20, 2013	David Hanners; Tad Vezner	Pioneer Press	Ch. 4, page 43
26.	Police Cleared in	September 20, 2013	Abby Simons;	Star Tribune	Ch. 4, page 43

			Matt McKinney		
	Franklin Death				
27.	Franklin Shot 10 Times, Autopsy Says	September 21, 2013	Matt McKinney	Star Tribune	Ch. 4, page 43
28.	Ex-Cop Says Firing Not Justified	January 12, 2014	Dave Chanen	Star Tribune	Ch. 6, page 48
29.	Independent Review of Minneapolis Police Department to Be Released	October 8, 2014	Boua Xiong	KARE, Channel 11 (NBC)	Ch. 6, page 52
30.	Minneapolis Mayor: Some Police Officers "Abuse the Trust"	October 9, 2014	Libor Jany	Star Tribune	Ch. 6, page 52
31.	White S.C. Officer Charged in Fatal Shooting of Black Man	April 8, 2015	Bruce Smith	Associated Press	Ch. 7, page 54
32.	Citizens' Videos Raise Questions on Police Claims	April 9, 2015	No Byline	New York Times	Ch. 7, page 54
33.	Use of Police Force is Poorly	May 1, 2015	Michael Wines	New York Times; Sarah	Ch. 7, page 56

	Tracked			Cohen	
34.	Rahm Handles Video the "Chicago Way"	December 3, 2015	John Kass	Chicago Tribune	Ch. 11, page 106
35.	Minnesota Officer Acquitted in Killing of Philando Castile	June 16, 2017	Mitch Smith	New York Times	Ch. 12, page 117
36.	Turbulent Year Challenges Mayor Hodges' Path Toward "One Minneapolis"	January 2, 2016	Erin Golden; Glen Stubbe	Star Tribune	Ch. 12, page 120
37.	Minneapolis Mayor Hodges Had 90 Minutes' Notice on Police Chief's Pick for 4th Precinct	April 29, 2017	Adam Belz; Dave Chanen	Star Tribune	Ch. 12, page 120
38.	Police report: Dogs "Charged at Officer" Before Being Shot in Mpls. Yard	July 11, 2017	Paul Walsh	Star Tribune	Ch. 12, page 121

39.	Australian Woman Shot and Killed by Minneapolis Police	July 17, 2017	Fred Melo; Nick Woltman	Pioneer Press	Ch. 12, page 121
40.	Officials: Australian Woman Shot After Cops Heard Loud Sound	July 18, 2017	Amy Forliti	Associated Press	Ch. 12, page 122
41.	Rosario: Another Fatal Shooting Here Begs for Answers – Twin Cities	July 18, 2017	Ruben Rosario	Pioneer Press	Ch. 12, page 123
42.	Where Justine Damond Died, Cameras Rolled too Late	July 19, 2017	Jon Tevlin	Star Tribune	Ch. 12, page 123
43.	Justine Damond Shooting: Officer Heard "Loud Sound" Before Partner Shot Minneapolis	July 19, 2017	Nick Woltman	Pioneer Press	Ch. 12, page 124

	Woman, BCA Says				
44.	Family of Woman Killed by Police Hires Attorney in Similar Minn. Case	July 20, 2017	Steve Karnowski; Amy Forliti	Associated Press	Ch. 12, page 122
45.	Woman "Slapped" Squad Car Before Justine Damond Police Shooting, Warrant Says	July 21, 2017	Amy Forliti	Associated Press	Ch. 12, page 124
46.	Justine Damond "Didn't Have to Die", Says Minneapolis Police Chief Janeé Harteau	July 21, 2017	Andy Mannix; Emma Nelson	Star Tribune	Ch. 12, page 125
47.	Body Camera Video Released of Minneapolis Police Officer Shooting Dogs in Backyard	July 20, 2017	Paul Walsh; Sarah Jarvis	Star Tribune	Ch. 12, page 125
48.	Chief Harteau	July 26,	Libor Jany;	Star	Ch. 12, page

	is Forced Out	2017	Andy Mannix; Eric Roper	Tribune	125
49.	Search of Justine Damond's Home Draws Scrutiny in Southwest Minneapolis	August 12, 2017	Adam Belz	Star Tribune	Ch. 12, page 126
50.	Freeman to Activists: No Evidence to Prosecute Officer in Justine Damond Shooting	December 15, 2017	Brandon Stahl	Star Tribune	Ch. 12, page 126
51.	Freeman Called a Grand Jury in Ruszczyk Killing. Why?	January 25, 2018	Riham Feshir	MPR News	Ch. 12, page 128
52.	Minneapolis Police Officer Mohamed Noor Turns Himself in on Murder, Manslaughter Charges in Justine Damond	March 21, 2018	Libor Jany	Star Tribune	Ch. 12, page 128

	Killing				
53.	Wrongful-Death Lawsuit from Police Shooting Can Proceed After Supreme Court Refuses City of Minneapolis Appeal	October 29, 2018	Libor Jany	Star Tribune	Ch. 13, page 142
54.	Video Shows Jailer Kneeing, Punching Handcuffed Black Man	February 25, 2019	Tom Lyden	KMSP, Channel 9 (FOX)	Ch. 14, page 143
55.	Experts Analyze Use of Excessive Force by Deputies at Minnesota Jail	February 25, 2019	Tom Lyden	KMSP, Channel 9 (FOX)	Ch. 14, page 143

Made in the USA
Columbia, SC
20 August 2021